MINIMALIST HOME

Learn How to Quickly Declutter Your Home, Organize Your Workspace, and Simplify Your Life to Have a Minimalist Lifestyle Using Minimalism Mindset & Habits

**By
Jenifer Scott**

Copyright 2019 by Jenifer Scott - All rights reserved.

This book is provided with the sole purpose of providing relevant information on a specific topic for which every reasonable effort has been made to ensure that it is both accurate and reasonable. Nevertheless, by purchasing this book you consent to the fact that the author, as well as the publisher, are in no way experts on the topics contained herein, regardless of any claims as such that may be made within. As such, any suggestions or recommendations that are made within are done so purely for entertainment value. It is recommended that you always consult a professional prior to undertaking any of the advice or techniques discussed within.

This is a legally binding declaration that is considered both valid and fair by both the Committee of Publishers Association and the American Bar Association and should be considered as legally binding within the United States.

The reproduction, transmission, and duplication of any of the content found herein, including any specific or extended information will be done as an illegal act regardless of the end form the information ultimately takes. This includes copied versions of the work both physical, digital and audio unless express consent of the Publisher is provided beforehand. Any additional rights reserved.

Furthermore, the information that can be found within the pages described forthwith shall be considered both accurate and truthful when it comes to the recounting of facts. As such, any use, correct or incorrect, of the provided information will render the Publisher free of responsibility as to the actions taken outside of their direct purview. Regardless, there are zero scenarios where the original author or the Publisher can be deemed liable in any fashion for any damages or hardships that may result from any of the information discussed herein.

Additionally, the information in the following pages is intended only for informational purposes and should thus be thought of as universal. As befitting its nature, it is presented without assurance regarding its prolonged validity or interim quality. Trademarks that are mentioned are done without written consent and can in no way be considered an endorsement from the trademark holder.

TABLE OF CONTENTS

Introduction 1
Chapter 1 *What Minimalism Is & Isn't* 3
Chapter 2 *Make A Plan* 6
Chapter 3 *Declutter & Organize The Kitchen* 12
Chapter 4 *Declutter The Dining Area* 15
Chapter 5 *Declutter & Organize The Bath Areas* 17
Chapter 6 *Declutter The Living Room* 20
Chapter 7 *Revamp The Office & Your Budget* 24
Chapter 9 *For Kids Only — Minimalism* 42
Chapter 10 *Declutter Laundry Spaces* 46
Chapter 11 *Clean & Organize Spare Storage Areas* 47
Chapter 12 *Methods Of Containment & Removal* 49
Chapter 13 *Benefits Of A Minimalistic Home* 52
Chapter 14 *The Minimalist Mindset* 56
Chapter 15 *The Minimalist Plan For Home Maintenance* 58
Chapter 16 *Natural Cleaning Supplies* 62
Conclusion *Maintain A Minimalistic Viewpoint* 85
Description 86

INTRODUCTION

Congratulations on purchasing *Minimalist Home: Learn How to Quickly Declutter Your Home, Organize Your Workspace, and Simplify Your Life to Have a Minimalist Lifestyle Using Minimalism Mindset & Habits*, and thank you for doing so!

This book contains proven steps and strategies on how to become a truly excellent organizer in a short time period. I'm not so sure about the "short" part, but the process does work. For example, how many times have you misplaced your keys? It's probably more times than you care to admit! Why not place a hook next to the door as the designated home for your keys?

Here's an inescapable fact: there's nothing worse than coming home from a hard day at work to view your home as a disaster area. You'll be surprised how easy it really is to get your home organized, where everything is in its proper spot.

It truly begins with a blueprint of what you plan will be to become a minimalist. It can start as simple as gathering and maintaining the inflow of clutter! Give yourself a 2-week cleanup excursion. You can always add a few days, but getting motivated is the first step.

If you need to have the carpets cleaned, you will need to add more time to your plan. However, since you have taken the incentive to get your home truly organized, why not have the professionals do the job for you?

Ask yourself a couple of questions: How long since you used the item—a week, a month? Where does the item belong, and does it have a specific space where it belongs? Does the item have a purpose not covered by another belonging? While it may seem that reducing clutter in your life is an impossible task, you unquestionably *can* do it.

Start right now by addressing your personal belongings—using baby steps. Conduct your research for a supportive community, and stay motivated by anticipating the conclusion you desire.

Does the item get in your way? Do I have space for the item? Your feelings are important, but they shouldn't trump the fact that you don't have the space to accommodate them. By overcrowding, you are causing the things you love to suffer.

Does the item in question bring you joy? You must be the one to decide, as a minimalist. Don't get lost in the fear and anxiety.

Do you find yourself saying, "But what if I need this someday?" Instead, think of it this way: "What do I need now?" At that point, "I know that I can't predict the future, and I also don't want to carry around every item imaginable for the next thirty years on the off chance I end up needing it. I put my <u>trust in the universe</u> that I will be able to get what I need, when I need it, from this moment onward."

Remember that simplifying the way you live, as well as minimizing the number of items in your living space, is just the first step for minimalist living. The process is not one to make you feel deprived—but to make you see the satisfaction you can derive with a less cluttered space.

It is essential as a minimalist to evaluate and adjust your style. In a nutshell, always remember true joy and contentment is what you desire—not a bunch of stuff that has no special space in your life. Continue the process and adjust the target goals as they develop over time. Do what you can at the moment using the tools you have acquired.

You will be cleaning and clearing the clutter using natural cleaning products—no more worrying about whether it's safe or not. Make it yourself, and you will know for sure. You will also find a couple of pleasing aromas throughout the book using essential oils.

Each segment is full of information to inform you of how to become a professional in terms of minimalism. I hope each method of organization will help you enjoy your home to its fullest.

"As you simplify your life, the laws of the universe will be simpler; solitude will not be solitude, poverty will not be poverty, nor weakness weakness."
—*Henry David Thoreau*

CHAPTER 1
What Minimalism Is & Isn't

Minimalism is having a vivid perception of what you value most in your life. You could believe it relates to items consuming your space and time. Minimalism is an *intentional* way that you live and allowing just what coordinates with your essential values to engulf your time and space. Minimalism is an individual choice. Each value is personal and unique to you. You must decide what's most important—and then discard anything that does not support those values.

Kill the Myths

Minimalism means you need to get rid of everything you own.
This is very untrue. It is about making more room for more of what matters in life—more space, more time, more freedom, and more peace.

Minimalism and frugality are just alike.
Frugality involves seeking opportunities to save money as you use caution to purchase less and shop with intentions of not overspending. At the same time, the primary intention of minimalism revolves around being frugal as well.
However, they are similar since both uphold the *intention* of how your money is spent. Minimalism is about living with less. Therefore, you have the essential space and time for everything else, which is most important in your life. Not all minimalists are focused on being frugal since they're willing to purchase higher quality items, which results in costing more money than other choices.

Minimalism makes life harder with its restrictions.
Many believe you need to get rid of all belongings except for the bare essentials, which would indeed make life harder. Not true! Life as a minimalist, you will spend much less time cleaning, looking for lost items, picking up, maintaining your stuff, organizing your stuff, and the list continues. Why? Because you do not have the additional stuff.
After you adopt a minimalist mindset, you will see that the belongings you believed made life simpler, are occupying essential space. Minimalism isn't centered on the removal of your items *if they* make your life easier and also are frequently used items. It's about removing all of the clutter of non-useful items.

Minimalism means an uninviting home.
Generally, minimalist design is aesthetic, and many times is symbolized by all-white rooms using minimal furniture or décor. There is another side to

the coin. You can decorate with colorful pillows, throw blankets, books, candles, and other decorative items you *cherish*.

Make the spaces personal and unique to you. Once again, your ideas will be different, allowing you to find the right amount of stuff for *you*. You set the limits of what limitations you place on the items. The key is just to keep what adds value to your life. Discard the remainder of the clutter. That's minimalism!

Minimalism only applies to your belongings.
Minimalism can be applied to all spheres of your life. Once you have a firm grasp of the idea of minimalism; you'll see how a minimalist lifestyle exceeds the decluttering your house. It can be applied on the basis of how you spend your time as well as what you eat.

You can't have a hobby with collections if you're a minimalist.
As a minimalist, you don't need to discard all of your belongings. You just become more intentional about what you keep by eliminating your possessions down to only the items you love and use.

Simply stated, learn moderation. Instead of owning 20 collections, just settle for two that you have a true passion for and enjoy. Stock only items you will use—be honest with yourself.

You must follow specific rules or standards as a *true* minimalist.
Create your own set of rules and alter the guidelines as your life changes. Be prepared for the challenging experience. It can open your mind to new ideas but don't be turned off or restricted by these rules. Work at it and discover the methods that work for you; not what doesn't. Remember, minimalism is identifying what you value most and removing all of the junk that doesn't match your new values.

What to Avoid — The Reasons You May Fail
1. *Procrastination*: Don't put off today and wait until tomorrow. The problems in your budget will not go away unless you stay on top of them constantly, and neither will the clutter created by the purchases. Stop finding excuses to deal with it later.
2. *No Perspective*: Some individuals do not think of his/her spending habits in the long-term. You begin to believe retirement is in the distant future, and the month-to-month money is sufficient. Unfortunately, this isn't the case. You lose perspective when you begin keeping all of your valuable possessions. Once again, you are making excuses for why the items are in such disarray.
3. *You Possess Poor Management Skills:* It is possible to reach an imbalance in your daily scheduling and many times overcommit your time.

4. *Short-Term Perspective*: Some people don't think of daily spending habits as wrong. He/she is not thinking of 20 to 30 years from now. Remember, more is less, and that includes your freedom instead of more objects in your life.
5. *Not Educated On Finances:* Many just do not know the difference between living day-to-day and saving for the future. The money is in the here and now; have fun! You can still have fun by planning your budget limitations.
6. *Living in the Past*: You need to remove the yearning for holding onto objects because they envelop you into a special memory. You have become sentimental to many attachments that are otherwise worthless to anyone else. Take a snapshot and let the item leave the house. Don't have an unbreakable bond or obligation for that pair of pants because it was a gift or keeping that beat up purse because it belonged to your Grandmother.

Let's make a blueprint of the future!

"It is a preoccupation with possession, more than anything else, that prevents men from living freely and nobly." —Bertrand Russell

CHAPTER 2
Make A Plan

Before making a plan, get your family onboard.

Create a Record of Your Goals

Remember balance and a simple budget can lower your stress, and that is another plus that cannot be ignored in the scheme of budgeting. Use a worksheet such as this one:

Short-Term Goals (Under 6 months)	Cost (Estimated)	Target Date	Save Weekly (Amount Needed)

Medium-Term Goals (6 months-1 year)	Cost (Estimated)	Target Date	Save Weekly (Amount Needed)

Long-Term Goals (Over 1 Year)	Cost (Estimated)	Target Date	Save Weekly (Amount Needed)

Estimate the costs to reach each of the goals. If you are not sure, do some research. You need to set a reasonable date. Don't set a date that will send your budget in a direction you cannot achieve. Determine the amount you need to make by dividing the estimated cost of your first goal by the number of weeks. That is the amount required. You must be ruthless when you make the cuts. Prioritize when you make the budget, but the planning starts here.

Create the Plan

You will create a long-lasting space for your belongings and follow techniques to help you return an item back where it belongs after it's used. Before you get going, you should first understand the importance of decluttering.

Clutter is paralyzing. Many folks are paralyzed in their tracks when looking at the stacks of paper on a desk or a messy pantry. The answer is; those individuals have *no idea* what to do next. As a result, many of the times, nothing is done. Your brain has difficulties differentiating between what's important and what's not. Generally, clutter will impede your ability to focus.

Decluttering will make you more efficient. You can move forward with your day quickly if you know where all your possessions are located when needed. For example, if your desk is organized with just what you need, tasks such as paying bills will consume much less time. Remember the formula, "Decluttering = More Time."

Clutter can create stress. Studies have indicated that those who walk into a cluttered environment (women in particular); his/her cortisol, your stress hormone levels will zoom. Therefore, you might not consciously realize it, but the disastrous cluttered space is causing anxiety.

Clutter will cause you to waste your time. Eliminating clutter could reduce household cleaning by approximately 40%. Your brain reads the cluttered environment signals that your work is never done. Subconsciously, your mind is preparing a huge to-do list that will continue to play over and over again in your mind.

There Is a Huge Link Between Physical Clutter and Mental Clutter

Clutter comes in all sizes and shapes, including the monstrous mental clutter which can be caused by the overstimulation created by the cluttered space you occupy.

Help Resolve Your Mental Clutter: Use L.I.V.E (List, Internal Organization, Vision and External Organization)
- **List**: Write it down, or you take a huge chance of forgetting it.
- **Internal Organization**: You must begin the organization process inside yourself first.
- **Vision**: You must be absolutely clear about what you want for your life in conjunction with your goals and all elements you want to attract into your lifetime.
- **External Organization**: You now may be organized internally and know where you are going and why. The next step in the process will be to start organizing your external environment.

For many, a daily calendar is essential for accurate time management. Schedule everything in your planner, including personal time events. Write down all of your to-do items on paper and make it a priority to keep it updated. Set the goals for one week, one month, and so forth.

Set limits and stick with it! Consider using some of the time you cut out for getting chores done. Ask for answerability from someone you trust if you're having issues concerning procrastination and getting tasks done.

You have made a huge step toward having a minimalistic home because you have decided; it is time to declutter your entire living space. You have noticed your closet is overstuffed. Your living spaces are cluttered with toys, books, and magazines. The bathroom cabinet is confusing, and the cabinets are totally cluttered. But, the question arises of where to start. Start at the top and work to the bottom.

Where to Begin

This guide will enable you to understand the process better. The professionals suggest preparing three boxes before you begin—one for articles to toss—one to donate—and one for the small items you wish to keep. Prepare a laundry basket for the relocation of gathered the items throughout the house.

The process begins by organizing each room. It's impossible to organize your items when you don't have a clue where to search. You can use a clothes basket or a box to move items from one room to the next. You can save many steps using this process.

It is best to remove all of the items you no longer use or need any more proceeding room by room before you begin to think about cleaning. It isn't unusual to find a Christmas decoration hiding until July.

Pull all of the throw rugs, floor mats, and runners throughout the house, and decide what can be washed and which ones need further cleaning. Even if you don't allow shoes in the house, a lot of dirt travels no matter what. These are some of the ways to start the new journey for the rest of your life:

Tip 1: The Honest Policy: Begin with honesty about what expenses are essential and the ones that are the 'like' or 'want' category. If you can remove a car payment or reduce rent/mortgage – now is a good time to start. Do you need all of the insurance premiums? Can you survive with one car or one that can be purchased outright with cash? Be Honest!

Tip 2: Seek Free Entertainment: Many of the local libraries offer free videos and books for your enjoyment. Consider using them versus the expense of visiting the theater. Go online, either at home or the library and find free community events you and your family can enjoy. Go to the local museum and search for programs and events in your town. Find a walking trail and spend time walking. Besides, it is excellent for your health! Volunteer as an usher at local plays and concerts to have a free ticket. All it will take is a short training period. Visit the zoo during the off-season or look for free days.

Tip #3: Prepare for the Unexpected. If you can take a second job for the short term, you could remove your debts much faster. It does not need to be a fast-paced position. Consider delivering pizza or online positions whereby you could use the Internet, which would justify the additional expense of the Internet. It would be useful and considered a 'need' instead of an entertainment item.

Paint the Picture: What the Minimalist Home Looks Like

- *You will see just essentials in the home.* Always be critical and ask yourself if the item (from a vase to furniture) is essential or if you can live without it. Go ahead, and strip the room down to the basics. Remove it from the space and enjoy the extra breathing room.
- *You will see quality over quantity as a minimalist trait*: Instead of having many items in your house, you would see items used most frequently. A comfortable, nice chair is better than six units of pressboard furniture.
- *Select one room to decorate at a time.* Make one room the center of calm. Use it as an inspiration to move onto the next room and the next.
- *Clear all of the floor space.* Don't stack any crates or boxes in the space. Once your furniture is down to the bare essentials, go ahead and remove everything else. Toss it into the trash or donate it. Just remove it from eyesight.
- *Furniture Usage Should Be Minimal:* You will only see a few essential items of furniture in a minimalist home. A living room may have a couch or loveseat, end tables, a couple of lamps, a minimalist entertainment stand, and a television. It could even contain less. A bedroom might have a functional bed (nothing fancy), a dresser, and perhaps a nightstand, and discard the rest of the clutter.
- *Clear surfaces are evident in a minimalistic home.* Flat surfaces are clear, except for a couple of special decorations.
- *Clear walls do provide serenity.* Display two or three favorite items of nice artwork. A minimalist will indulge in a simple photo, painting, or drawing framed with a solid color on each wall to eliminate boredom. It's perfectly fine to leave some of the walls bare.
- *Accent On Decorations.* Display a few items on a coffee table or have a clear desk with just a have a family photo.
- Turn on some music to get you motivated and get your adrenaline pumping. This is a basic guideline of how to proceed:

How to Declutter Any Room?

Step 1: Choose a space, preferably in the middle of the room. If you are in a room with tables or any other surface, you can also use that for placing items.

Step 2: Start on one side of the room and work around the entire room.
Step 3: Don't jump around! Do one shelf, drawer, or closet section at a time.
Step 4: Pull everything out/off of the drawer/shelf in the designated space.
Step 5: Clean the drawer/shelf and set it aside.
Step 6: Sort into the keep, donate or toss pile. Make quick choices but look at each item. Be honest: when is the last time you used the item?
Tip: When in doubt, throw it out is a good logic to maintain as you declutter your living spaces. However, seasonal items are the exception to the logic of not keeping items if you have not used them at least once in six months.
Step 7: Move to the next shelf or drawer or segment of the floor.
With an organized movement during the sorting stage, you will appreciate the touch-up day. Use each chapter of this book for its designed use. The plans are based on a room to room method, just as a basis of how you could do the whole house without missing a single area. You may choose to perform the clean and decluttering process at the same time.
After cleaning, and discarding the clutter from just one space should give you a feeling of euphoria involved with the minimalistic way of living.

Benefits of Keep-Toss-Donate Containers

The containers keep the plan organized. During the sorting process, give yourself just a few seconds to consider your choice. If it takes longer than that time, you probably don't need the item. Another great tip; use dark trash bags, so you aren't tempted to retrieve any of the items.
Consider how much you can be helping others by donating items. You could be providing a coat for someone who doesn't have a coat for winter or a child that doesn't have any toys. What about donating some of the items your family doesn't use to a homeless shelter?
Don't think about how sad you might be by eliminating so many knick-knacks and books. Look at the amount of time you will save by not needing to pick up and dust them every week. Spend that time with your family and friends.

Items Are Just Items

If you are holding onto items because someone you care about gave them to you; you can still get rid of them. Take a picture to save the memory and let the object go. Keep the items you believe are heirlooms but let the rest leave home. It will clear the space for contentment. You will always share the memory in your mind and in the photo.
Here is a list of some of the items many people don't believe are clutter:
- Broken sunglasses
- Outdated eyeglasses
- Pens without ink (never checked)
- Poor-fitting clothes

- Mismatched socks
- Poor-fitting shoes
- Condiment packages of ketchup, mustard, etc.
- Plastic silverware
- Rubber bands
- Magazines over 2 months
- Week old newspapers
  The list can go on for an eternity of the items you 'might' need. Did you see anything in there that you recognized? The rule of thumb is; if you haven't used it within the last year, it should be donated, consigned, or trashed.

Appraise the Item's Value

Sometimes, sentiments take over, but take a picture and remove the clutter! Try the box and banish routine. If you are tugging with certain items; place them in a box and label them with destroy; tape and date the box. One year later, if you haven't opened the box—take it to a donation center without opening the seal. If you believe later you made a mistake, it is done, and you had claimed the sentiment already when you sealed the box.

You are probably asking, 'what about the true value?' In that case, you need to learn the rules for value by example. An associate has some old computers that he/she believes are valuable. You must consider a computer is not going to be valued even close to what you paid for it when it was new. If you believe you have something of monetary value, set it aside, and ask the dealer. If that is your only excuse (it's valuable), it is time to be placed into the donation box or trash bin.

"Simplicity is the ultimate sophistication." —Leonardo da Vinci
Let's continue!

CHAPTER 3
Declutter & Organize The Kitchen

It is a pretty good chance your kitchen cabinets can use a good clean out. Before you get started, it's a good idea to have the kitchen space in somewhat of an ordinary state.

Fill the dishpan with hot, soapy water for a quick clean-up or removal of dust from some of the items. Also, empty the dishwasher for the dirty items found in the cabinets. Save a step, place the dirty item directly into the dishwasher or dishpan.

As you collect items into the different boxes of the 'keep' items, try to sort them accordingly in groups so it will be simpler after you finish the cleaning to replace them to the proper space or area. Use some of these tips to get you going:

Declutter & Clean Out the Refrigerator

Begin at the top of the refrigerator and remove everything. Clean out each shelf as you proceed. If any of the drawers or shelves are removable, take each unit out, and use warm soapy water to clean it. You want to clean every surface, especially the ones on the door—inside and out.

Before placing your food back inside of the fridge, line the shelves with some parchment paper or plastic food wrap to make cleaning a breeze. If you have a small mess, just remove the layer of plastic, and it is clean!

Organize the Cabinets

If you are an avid cook, consider installing a retractable book stand. Your recipe will be at eye level as you mix all of your ingredients and perform magic. When you are done, you take your clean (flour-free) book and place it in the clean bookcase. The holder is moved under the cabinet out of your way and view until you need it again.

The extra spaces in the cabinets can store the small appliances that previously cluttered the countertops. Only place frequently used items on the counter, such as a coffee maker.

Do store the toaster, toaster oven, food processors, and blenders inside or under the cabinet. Keep all of the food products out of sight. You can also store the canisters under the counter or in a pantry.

Remember, if the counter is clear—it's easy to clean!

Revamp the Pantry

It makes no difference whether you have a pantry or not; just update the space where you store your food items. You will be surprised how many items are no longer fresh. Be sure to check the dates located on each product.

Toss any of the empty boxes or boxes that just have a small portion of the product left in the package. For example, if you have half a bag of rice,

consider putting it into a covered container. This will also eliminate the chances of any bugs invading your space. You will also be able to find it the next time you need to use it.
Note: If your item needs directions; cut the directions from the package and tape it on the new container/jar.
It's important to check the dates on your spices because as seasoning makers including McCormick point out, the spices don't spoil, but the potency is lost with time. The intended flavor might not be what you expect if you use it in your recipe. It is a smarter choice to replace them regularly. This is a short list of how long some spices will last:
- Whole Black Peppercorns: 4 years
- Chili Powder: 3 to 4 years
- Dried Bay Leaves: 1 to 3 years
- Ground Ginger: 3 to 4 years
- Ground Cinnamon: 3 to 4 years
- Dried Oregano Leaves: 1 to 3 years
- Crushed Red Pepper: 2 to 3 years

Tip: Keep red spices such as chili powder, paprika, and other red peppers in the refrigerator to keep them fresh longer.

Beautify & Revamp the Pots & Pans
- Separate the pots from the pans.
- Store the tops separately.

If your décor is flexible; hang them on the wall as a decoration when not in use. When you begin to place your bakeware back into the cabinet, try using a storage divider, and stack the pan tops as well as the muffin tins.

Minimize the Utensils
- Take out each item and perform the process of keep-toss-donate-trash. You will probably find many duplicates and lots of bread ties.

Note: If your tongs no longer have a locking clasp; you can use the cardboard tube from an empty paper towel roll to keep the arms together!
- Everyday utensils can be stored in a wooden or plastic divider.
- Store all sharp knives separately to prevent injury.
- Trash any broken, stained, or extra unnecessary pieces.

Inventory the Dishes
Comb through the cabinets for any dishes which have become chipped or cracked.

Revitalize Tupperware & Similar Containers
- Match the tops and bottoms.
- Trash any stained containers.

Prepare an "In Doubt" Box
You have reached the middle ground of doubt! So many items that take a second thought could be the items that need to go out to the trash pile first. A good example is the electric French-fryer that has two-year-old grease caked on its surface. Let it go!

Oh, and the cute cake mold of the fifty states you baked (oh my) five years ago, and have not used since. Don't be sentimental now; let it go!

Suggestion: If you have a box of items which you aren't sure about, give yourself a test, stash the box of items for a month or so (just a small box). If you have not opened the box, you have answered your own question; donate the items.

The Kitchen Sink
It's time to tackle the kitchen sink. Just because you wash out the sink daily after you do a load of dishes, doesn't mean it is clean. Water spots, rust, soap scum, and food stains can build up if you don't stay ahead of them.

Porcelain Sinks: If you have a porcelain sink, you can make it gleam with this process:
1. Line the sink with paper towels.
2. Soak them with bleach.
3. Let them soak for 30 minutes, and discard them.
4. Rinse the sink with hot running water.

Note: Don't use bleach on colored porcelain because it will fade. Instead, use vinegar, baking soda, or a mild detergent (and a bit of elbow grease). Now that you have the sink clean, you can protect it from scratches and stains by installing a plastic mat on the bottom of the sink. The mat will protect the shiny sink from lingering acidic foods/liquids such as salad dressing, vinegar, and fruit.

CHAPTER 4
Declutter The Dining Area

There are more spaces to hide clutter than you can imagine in the confines of your dining space. If your home has a formal dining area as well as a breakfast nook, the dining room may not be used often for its purpose. It's a prime dumping ground for clutter.

Dining rooms tend to have storage pieces can include quite a collection of drawers and cabinets such as china cabinets or buffets. If you eat the majority of your meals at your kitchen island, you may have a tendency to store things there that you want to get out of sight.

Fancy serving pieces such as wedding gifts as well as other decorative items are easy to stash into the bottom of either cabinet, but you could be taking up valuable space you could be using to hold the items you actually use.

Gifts can be difficult to purge because of guilt but if you're not using the item, toss it. Donate it for someone who will use it, and be guilt-free. Just think how great you will feel when your dining room is tidy.

Put yourself to the test. Place a batch of questionable items into a storage box. If it hasn't opened in one or two months, it should be tossed. Set a reminder on your phone to check back in on it in two or three months. If you haven't missed it, it's probably safe to donate the item.

Make use of decorative baskets you already own to keep all items together or use a drawer organizer in our china cabinet drawer. Keep a few small storage boxes that make it easier to fold and store items such as your rectangular placemats.

The China Cabinet/Hutch/Buffet

Remove all items from the cabinet and clean it. Use a good wood cleaner to refresh the surface, naturally.

Take just five minutes to do a quick run in the china cabinet. You might be surprised what you end up with in your box of questionable items. Quickly, consider items you can easily part with and place them into a keep-toss-donate stack, so you are not tempted later to put the items back. Don't be tempted to put it in the attic!

It depends on how much silver you have, whether you clean it for now or wait until your 10-day tidy home plan is completed. Save the heirloom pieces and consider consigning, donating, or gifting the items.

When you enter your dining room, you want to see a clean table with a beautiful centerpiece. Imagine, the thought of it already put a smile on your face. When you walk into the dining room to a table full of clutter, you immediately feel stressed.

The 1-Touch Rule

Employ the 1-Touch rule in the dining area. As you're sorting through mail or coming into the house with a bunch of stuff, make it a goal to only touch the item one time before putting it in its proper space.

If it's unessential paperwork; just put it right in the trash or recycling bin. If it's groceries, just put them away right away.

By committing to only touching the item once, you are a lot less likely to have piles of stuff appearing all over the flat surfaces of our house! It can take a while to get into the habit of the 1-touch rule, but you may find the longer you aim to utilize it in the house, the more organized your home remains.

CHAPTER 5
Declutter & Organize The Bath Areas

Declutter/Organize the Bathrooms
Keep your goal in sight. You are attempting to maximize the bathroom space and make everything accessible and easily reached by all family members. Sometimes, it is not an easy task to find a one-plan-fits-all solution. However, these are some of the tips to help you with the process:

Group the Items
If you have a stockpile of products such as extra hair care products, group them together in an organized manner. If you have three partially used bottles of the same shampoo or conditioner, mix the similar products and toss/recycle the extra container. Be sure to check under the cabinet and in the shower stall.

Drawers: Remove all of the items from the bathroom drawers and place them in containers for sorting. If an item is obviously trash, throw it away immediately. At this point, don't linger on an item. Clean the drawer, so it can thoroughly dry overnight.

Countertops & Sinks: Use the same procedures as used in the kitchen space. It will depend on the material used on the sinks and countertops.

Medicine Cabinet Purge: You already have the medicine cabinet empty from giving it a thorough cleaning; now it's time to do the tedious job of checking the dates of the medicine from the cabinet. Throw away all expired prescriptions or over-the-counter medicines. If you have any ointments, also check for spoilage of them.

As crazy as it sounds, your medicine should not be stored in the bathroom because the vitamins and medicines can become damaged from the steam and heat from showers. Place them in the kitchen instead - just for safety purposes.

Store your antiseptics, bandages, gauze, or other first aid items in the medicine cabinet. You can use it to store extra swabs, nail clippers, or any smaller items. Consider placing your toothbrushes in the cabinet to keep them more sanitary.

Place a couple of hangers on the linen closet door for hanging blow dryers, curling irons, or extra towels. It all improves the appearance of the bathroom.

Regroup The Linen Closet: Go through the cabinet/linen closet and discard any torn or dingy towels or washcloths. You can reuse the damaged ones for cleaning rags. Remember Grandma's saying, 'Waste not; want not.' Store the extra toilet paper on the top shelf, out of the way of the regularly used items such as towels. You can also purchase a toilet paper stacker to save space.

Prepare an All-White Linen Closet
If your decluttering plan is part of the redecorating scheme; considering using all light color sheets, towels, and pillowcases. Designers believe it is more soothing to save the splashy colors for the throw pillows, blankets, and shower curtains; just a thought!
- **Hint:** If you have special linens and towels for guests; consider placing them in a plastic bin. Label them for easy access.

The Shower Curtain
It is beneficial to use a shower curtain liner made from cotton, hemp, synthetic, or vinyl. While you are deep cleaning, either replace the liner or machine wash it in hot water using a mild laundry detergent. Washing the liner weekly will help prevent the buildup of mold or mildew. If you prefer to hand-wash the liner, use ten parts of water to 1-part bleach.
Clean the outer shower curtain by following the manufacturer's instructions or in warm/hot water with a mild detergent.
Note: Leave the shower curtain closed when it is not being used so water cannot sit in the folds.

Limited Bathroom Space Solutions
If you are limited in space as many people are living in smaller homes, use an over the door shoe organizer. Purchase one that is clear, so you can place many items in the unit and know exactly where it is when it is needed.
Use a rule of thumb and corral any of the items that won't stack easily. Consider using small bins that can be stacked under the sink or in the drawers for makeup, and other small items that you can never find.
Place cotton swabs (Q-tips), cotton balls, and similar items in closed containers to keep them clean, organized, and out of the way.

Label the Shelves
If you have several shelves containing miscellaneous items, you can avoid a lot of digging/searching later. You can use masking tape or a label maker, to keep the children involved. Not only is it neater, but also a lot less time is spent with wondering where a certain item is when it is needed.

Refresh the Space
To finish off the bathroom space, add a box of baking soda in the corner of the closet to absorb any of the musty odors which can collect.

Corral the Children's Bath Toys
You can use several containers for the children's playtime adventures. You can use a milk crate or plastic laundry basket for the items. It will keep they neatly stored behind the shower curtain. If you want them hidden away in a closet, be sure they are completely dry to prevent mildew.

Under-the-Sink Storage

If you have limited space under the sink, it is probably best to remove everything first. Go through each article to decide if it's still needed; if not, toss it. Use a metal rack and store smaller things you may need in the lower section of the cabinet space. After you declutter, you can reorganize all the stuff. Put away the items that do not belong there. Just remember, you will need to quickly remove the items if you have a plumbing emergency. That's why it's important not to have it packed to the max.

CHAPTER 6
Declutter The Living Room

It is unbelievable how disorganized a living room or den can become in such a short amount of time. Here are a few tips to be sure you cover all of the areas where clutter might be taking over your living space without you realizing the problem.

You will want to begin with the same boxes for keep-toss-donate-or trash. It is easier if you wipe each of the 'keep' items while you have it in your hands. If you have children, include them in on the action. You might not mean it but play a game/trick and inform him/her if their belongings aren't out of the collection boxes in fifteen minutes; they will be gone. It might not work, but you tried! The point is to remove everything from the space that doesn't belong.

Books & Magazines

Quickly, sort through the clutter of magazines and books that have accumulated and discard, recycle, or donate the ones you have already read. Place the books on the bookshelves after you have wiped down the covers.

The secret to magazines is learning when you have enough of them. If you have a huge stack, maybe you should reconsider rejecting the renewal except for your favorite ones (not all of them)!

Consider donating the discarded magazines and books to a nursing home facility or retirement home. Some of the books might be considered for donation to local schools, libraries, or even to correctional facilities. At any rate, you need them out of your house.

Sorting the Shelves

Comb through each shelf and decide how many knickknacks you really need on one shelf. The 'dust-collectors' are so cute on the shelf in the store but can make clutter quickly. Of course, it doesn't mean you need to toss Grandma's favorite teacup. Within reason, keep the cherished ones or consider passing them on down the generation line to achieve a clean and clear atmosphere in your space.

Browse through all of the movies and DVDs. Eliminate any empty cases that don't have a use anymore. You can recycle them or donate them along with the movies you won't be viewing again. Discard any damaged or scratched movies.

Sort through all of the end tables, and remove any garbage, loose papers, or unnecessary items. Use your keep-toss-donate boxes to stay organized. Remember; don't think about the item except momentarily.

Rearrange the Book Shelves
You can make a bookcase more presentable if you remove all of the covers that are tattered and torn and place them elsewhere. You want to place focus on serenity, and you cannot do that if you are looking at the ragged edges of a book.

You can achieve an attractive backdrop by using a little bit of paint or adding some wallpaper to your space. Mix some round vases or pictures into the scenery next to a column of your nicely organized special books. Mix and match until you have a unique setting fit for a showroom.

Many organizers believe you should use one-third accessories, one-third books, and one-third empty spaces. Mix the shelves with 60% of the books placed vertically and 40% placed horizontally to create both spontaneity and balance. The point is not to make it too busy.

Take a picture in your mind or one on the phone to remind yourself of how good everything looks right now. Every three to six months, take the books down and dust the tops and spines. Flip through the pages and rotate the books to prevent any warping.

If you want to add some new dazzle to the area, consider adding some battery-operated candles to accent your newly arranged space.

Maintain the Kid's Toys
Children's toys will require some teamwork. Go back to the keep-toss-donate
boxes, and keep them handy. If your children are older, let them help with the process. If not, it might be easier to do the job—solo. Make a choice by deciding if they are toys or items the children use actively.

If they are for a younger age group, it's best to remove them from your space. Of course, you don't need to throw away the Three Bears book. However, you can place it into the bookcase instead of the toy box. (More on kids later.)

Walls - Stairs & Landings
The walls should be wiped down with warm soapy water. Don't forget to clean the baseboards. You can see dust bunnies across any room!

If you have any stairs or landings in your home, you will need to thoroughly clean each step with a whisk broom, a hand-held vacuum or a damp rag. If there are carpet sections, be sure to get along the edges thoroughly.

For all handrails and pickets; wipe each individual piece and around the bottom to remove any dirt that might have been captured.

For all spaces, use the crevice tool and brush attachment to remove the debris from the edges of the wall/baseboards.

Oil Stains on Carpet: If you have carpeted areas that have oil stains; you can use cat litter or baking soda on it to absorb the oil. Even professionals use this process.

Clean All Ceiling Fans

If you have ceiling fans, the living room is the best place to start. Since you are cleaning the house from top to bottom; it is best to pull out the vacuum cleaner hose and the broom to remove all of the cobwebs from the ceilings. Don't forget to check the fan since it will be circulating clean, fresh air. A dusty fan can ruin all of your hard work. The process only takes about fifteen minutes.

To clean the blades, this is all you need to do:
- *Step 1:* Tape the fan's switch for safety, so it doesn't accidentally get turned on while you clean the blades.
- *Step 2:* Place some old sheets or a drop cloth on the floor and remove any furniture under the fan. The blanket/drop cloth should cover a radius of approximately two that of the blades of the fan.
- *Step 3:* Use a spray bottle filled with water and 2 Tablespoons of distilled white vinegar. Spray the inside of an old/damaged pillowcase and place it under each fan blade.
- *Step 4:* Cover your head with a baseball cap.
- *Step 5:* Stand on a ladder to place your head above the blades.
- *Step 6:* Slip the pillowcase over each blade to remove the bulk of the dust.
- *Step 7:* Use a clean cloth to dust the lingering dust and the light fixture.

Be sure to perform these steps before you vacuum the floors.

The Heating/AC Vents

Check the heating vents, and remove any buildup of dust in each space of the home. Change the filter.

As preventive maintenance, once each month:
- Vacuum the unit with the crevice tool.
- Remove the cover and soak it in soapy water.
- Scrub it with a soft brush.

Remember to have the ductwork cleaned out about every three to five years.

Clean the Couches & Chairs

If you aren't sure, the fabric of your couch the manufacturer should have a label somewhere indiscreetly sewn into the seam of the fabric. Check underneath the cushions or the base of the furniture. You should see a label with some of the following descriptions:
- *SW:* Water or Solvent cleaner is safe to use.
- *W:* Okay to use water for cleaning.
- *S:* Use only solvent-based cleaners.
- *X:* Use Only the Vacuum for cleaning.

Once you have decided how to proceed with the type of cleaner, use this process to clean the soiled couch or chair.

- *Step 1:* Use a brush or white cleaning rag to groom the entire space to help remove any dried-on spots of food or other debris.
- *Step 2:* Sprinkle a large amount of baking soda over the entire couch. The soda will help to absorb any nasty smells and helps break up any stains lingering in the fabric.
- Wait for 20 minutes to an hour before you use the brush attachment of your vacuum cleaner to sweep away the powder.
- *Step 3:* Clean the sofa with the below cleaner if needed.

Cleaning Tip: Be sure to test an unnoticeable spot before you spray the entire sofa.

CHAPTER 7
Revamp The Office & Your Budget

"Too many people spend money they haven't earned, to buy things they don't want, to impress people they don't like." —Will Rogers

The office is a space that seems to collect a lot of extra papers to look at 'later,' but sometimes, later doesn't happen. You need to become diligent and dive into the disaster one piece of paper at a time.

You might need to compile a box of questionable materials that might require a bit of concentration, such as the directions for the cable box. It isn't an item you need right away, but it's something that needs to be filed away. However, don't set it aside as part of the clutter/hoard to be discovered years later during another clean-up time. Look through the box while you are watching television, or between the commercials. Diligently, comb through all of the files and eliminate any unnecessary information. Any documents with your personal information should be immediately shredded if you don't need them, such as old identification cards or similar information.

Quickly, look over the receipts to see if they are over a year old—if so, toss them. If you are saving them for tax purposes, place them in a specific folder, and file them.

Bills over one-year-old should be thrown away. A paper shredder is excellent for destroying the documents to help prevent identity fraud. Place everything back into the desk in an organized manner. If you don't have any desk organizers for the drawers, you can use some of the plastic containers from the kitchen that didn't have tops. You won't feel as wasteful. Later on, when you purchase an organizer, simply throw the containers away, or recycle them with no guilt!

Electronics & the Computer

Your computer keyboard and mouse, as well as your phone, are other excellent spaces that need to be cleaned regularly and thoroughly. Think of all of the spaces where bacteria can grow. Never use abrasive cleaners on any of the products. Always unplug the item before attempting to clean it to prevent electrical damage. Get in the habit of cleaning them weekly as part of your anti-clutter/cleaning adventure.

Organize the Office

Remove as much paperwork clutter as possible. If you have piles of mail building up on your counter or desktop, it may be time to eliminate the source. Shift your account statements to online service. The correspondence will slow down immensely.

Join the crowd and go paperless. There are many options with the use of the Internet. Forget digging for a bill and do what many families are now using. Use one website such as File this or Evernote for your convenience. You are taking up less space and removing the paper clutter.

No Space for an Office? While you are in organization mode; do you have your information stored in boxes because of a lack of space? Consider using a rolling microwave cart to store your necessary items. When you are ready to pay the bills; just grab the cart and carry it where you want to sit. The cart is always neat and uncluttered. Use some decorative boxes for a décor improvement.

Purge the Paperwork: At the top of the list of decluttering; it begins with your disorganized and outdated files just taking up space in your bookcase or filing system. Saving unneeded papers only clutters the cabinet with items you don't need and no place for the ones you do need.

Try to weed your files down to one file cabinet drawer. If you have a scanner, put them online and throw the junk away. Consider keeping your tax receipts in a safe spot for references next year. Place it in with other papers, including your insurance information, birth certificates, and other vital documents. IRS only requires files for seven years back.

While You're in the Office

- Cancel all subscriptions to store coupons or emails. You want to eliminate temptations when possible.
- Tip 10: Magazines: Magazine subscriptions are another item that can probably keep your budget-strapped down. Do you let them pile up like most people? If so, this is how the 'clutter' theory works. Purchase them singly if you want to catch up or better yet; use the Internet with its free Wi-Fi.
- Batch bill payments. It is an excellent habit to pay your bills monthly. You won't need to worry about due dates. The time saved will reduce stress, and you won't feel like you do nothing but pay bills. What a relief that can be if you have a busy lifestyle.
- Online Banking: Many bank accounts can be handled online without needing to visit a brick-and-mortar. Rates are usually lower because you don't have the additional personnel that you need to face in a regular bank. You do not have to choose a bank branch that is close to your home; it is as close as your computer.
- Depositing Your Check: You can easily hide your check (from your conscious mind) by using several methods. You can use a remote check deposit by snapping a photo of the check and submitting it to the bank without leaving your home. Thus, you are not as tempted to go shopping and get other cute trinkets.
- Clean Computer Files: The computer will clutter your mind with endless garbage unless you remove it.
- Reduce Social Media Contacts: Analyze the way you use the content on your wall. Does the feed provide you with inspiration or with ways to benefit your life? If yes, keep the contact. If the answer is

no, remove the person or group. Negativity must go so minimalism can enter.

Regroup the Budget

If you are like many, you haven't got a clue where all your money has gone after the checks were deposited. Preparing a budget will allow you to spend as a minimalist and know where each hard-earned dollar has been spent. You must categorize by needs, wants, and likes or better known as luxuries. Identify your expenses using the past six months as a starting point. Be sure to include all family members when you make a list.

Needs: The lines become blurred with today's technological advances. The true basics are clean water, food, and a way to prepare it, shelter, warmth, and clothing. Unless an expense is required for your job, you don't actually need a cell phone, high-speed internet, or cable TV. Yes, that cable is a hard choice, but it really is a luxury. The lines are hard-drawn, but you have to be brutal when setting up a minimalist way of living.

Include all of the expenses such as food and water (to maintain your health), housing, transportation, and other essential needs, including healthcare and hygiene products. Consider clothing as a need, but only enough to remain appropriately dressed and comfortable.

According to the experts, a minimum repayment on a credit card is considered a need, and it could negatively affect your credit score (if minimum payments are not met). Needs are considered to be any payment if it can severely impact your life's quality, such as prescription medicines.

Wants: These are the items you desire to add to your budget plan but must be an item that is necessary to keep your other expenses at a minimum. It could include a new vehicle or an updated computer if needed for work (only if your computer is not working). A 'want' can also include back-to-school clothing.

Guidelines for a Spending Budget

As a minimalist, you will want to make room for happiness. Preparing a budget can eliminate the stress factor. Use these as a guideline to prepare your personal plan:

- Groceries – Essential items
- Grocery items beyond basic essentials
- Special Dining Out Events
- Bar fees
- Coffee
- Meals purchases at work or school
- Drinks and snacks purchased at school or work

Shelter Expenses

Utilities

- Water & Sewer
- Trash Pickup
- Electricity
- Gas for heating or Cooking
- Phone: Cell & Landline/Primary - residential phone
- Cable

Home Furnishings

- Remodeling or renovations
- Cell phone
- Satellite or cable TV
- High-speed Internet

Additional Savings – Emergency Funds

- Vehicle replacement fund
- Retirement
- Children's college fund
- Various financial goals

Personal Items

- Prescription medications
- Clothing & Clothing Maintenance
- Toiletries
- Salon Care: Haircuts, perms, color, massage

Gifting: Holiday, birthday, anniversary, wedding

Entertainment

- Video games
- Music Purchases
- Movie tickets
- Concerts
- DVD & movie rentals
- Books, newspaper and magazine subscriptions
- Vacations
- Health or other club memberships
- Parties: Birthday, holiday, social events

Pets

- Food

- Cat litter
- Veterinary care

Household Expenses

- Mortgage (1st or 2nd) and Rent
- Homeowners Insurance and Taxes or Renter's Insurance
- Homeowners Association Fees
- Repairs to the home
- Furniture
- House Cleaning Services
    - Domestic help: Babysitter, house cleaning help, pet sitters
    - Home maintenance: Exterminators, lawn care, painters

Family Expenses

- Children School and Activity Funds (if you have children)
- School Tuition and Books
- Day Care
- Child Support
- Alimony – Spousal support

Insurance Premiums

- Life
- Health
- Disability

Credit Payments – Minimum payments

- Card 1, 2, etc.
- Student Loans

Transportation

- Lease payment or automobile loan
- Vehicle usage and similar expenses for children
- Gasoline
- Automobile maintenance
- Tolls, public transportation, parking fees

Vehicle Expenses

- Car Payment
- Minimum fuel
- Vehicle Insurance

- Smog Check, License renewal, & taxes
- Repairs & Maintenance

Transportation/Miscellaneous

- Taxi service as needed
- Parking fees
- Tolls
- Bus/Subway fees

Once you have these expenses calculated; you have the totals of the items you 'want'. Then, subtract after-tax income. The total will exceed the surplus or shortfall of the money you will want to 'earmark' on your budget. If you don't have money for unexpected expenses, you may need to tighten up and discover new ways to increase your income levels. You may need to do a more diligent accounting of your 'needs' before you can receive a surplus for your wants.
Likes: This category is used for expenses of items that you wish to have but do not need them immediately. It can fall into a savings allotment, which will be discussed further in the following chapters.

Set Boundaries for Expenses Monthly

If you are on a fixed income, it is essential to designate where each dollar will be spent. Be sure to stick with it; meaning, don't decide mid-month to make a purchase not already noted in the budget's outline.
Teamwork is essential for the budget to be sufficient. You must also make your children stay within the guidelines. Of course, there may be times when you need to make purchases that are not planned for at the beginning of the month. In that case, you will need to extract money from another part of the budget, such as entertainment.
Learning how to make adjustments will take some 'give and take' from all family members. To begin, you will want to remain focused on the written budget on a daily basis. Once you have that mastered, check it weekly to be sure you are on the right path. When that is reached, the monthly plan will be easier to adjust.
By the second or third month, you should have a decent baseline of how you and your family are spending its money. Be consistent and pay your bills as they become due. You will enjoy the stress-free budgeting as you master how to live with your minimalist way of life.
Take five or ten minutes each week working with your budget. You will be surprised how quickly you can recognize the many ways you did not know you were overspending.
Once you have had a chance to monitor your expenses and income for a month or two, you'll be more aware of the areas you need to monitor more closely. Maybe your monthly expenses were way off, or maybe you did not

account for veterinary bills or car repairs. Once you have worked out the kinks, it is essential to follow it to the letter.

By following these easy guidelines, you will soon discover there is one critical element of minimalism, and that is persistence. Merely beat down the expenses to a minimum, and make the adjustments to empower your cash flow. Remember, no budget is forever. Periodic checks will enable you to review and stay on the right course to a successful financial future.

Simplify Your Finances

You are probably wondering how many accounts you need to remain organized. These are a few suggestions to get you started on the right path:

Maintain one (1) primary checking account. Use this account for bill payments only.

Keep only one (1) credit card (maybe 2). The card can be used as a financial tool, but be careful not to overspend. Remember that you will be paying interest on the money when you make the purchases. Even if it is a sale item, the interest payments may exceed the sale price. Think twice! This is a vital step toward becoming debt-free. American Express is an excellent choice since its fee is due monthly.

Open one main savings account. Use this for emergency goals or shortages that occur within your budget for the month. Use it only when it is a 'must have' item or an emergency.

Automate: Direct deposit is excellent, and you know your check will be there with no bank holds and no time is wasted for a trip to the bank for deposit. Use this for your car payment, mortgage, or any other bills you encounter. You can also transfer money to your savings account using online features. Make paying bills simpler.

Batch bill payments. It is an excellent habit to pay your bills monthly. You won't need to worry about due dates. The time saved will reduce stress, and you won't feel like you do nothing but pay bills. What a relief that can be if you have a busy lifestyle.

Join the crowd and go paperless. There are many options with the use of the Internet. Forget digging for a bill and do what many families are now using. Use one website such as File This or Evernote for your convenience. You are taking up less space and removing the paper clutter.

Consider debt consolidation. It is best to have all of your accounts in one place. Don't use the high-interest companies. Search online to find one that features zero or low-interest rates and consolidate. Save the money of having multiple fees.

Downsize your car if possible. Do you really need a 4x4 when a compact model would serve your needs? Think of the money saved that could be applied to other essential items in your budget.

Cancel all subscriptions to store coupons or emails. You want to eliminate temptations when possible.

Magazines: Magazine subscriptions are another item that can probably keep your budget strapped. Do you let them pile up like most people? If so,

this is how the 'clutter' theory works. Purchase them singly if you want to catch up or better yet; use the Internet with its free Wi-Fi.
Books: Purchasing books from the bookstore can be eliminated if you visit your local library. They are free. If you choose, you can also visit a thrift store or purchase them online for a minimal fee. Use the money from your entertainment fund, not the emergency fund.
Coffee, Tea, and Soda: If you are a gourmet coffee drinker and must have one for the office. Purchase an insulated mug and make your own at home. The same rings true if you believe that you must have to have a soda pop. Think of the savings if you work a full-time job.
Storage: If you have a storage unit, consider selling the items, unless they have sentimental value. Take a picture and add the money saved and proceeds of the sale to your emergency fund.
Most of all, you are eliminating stress and complications. You will be able to think of many other ways to get the ball rolling in the right direction to your savings potential. Clarity is the goal when you begin to use the minimalist budgeting techniques.

Reduce Your Utilities

You realize utilities such as gas or electric for heating purposes is going to be expensive. Sometimes, no matter how much you have in your budget, it doesn't seem to be enough. You can help remove some of the stress and discover new ways to live a minimalist lifestyle without breaking the bank and your nerves.

Heating Costs

Consider some of these ways to reduce your heating costs:
Free Solar Heating: Open those blinds and curtains. Let the sun keep your home warm during daylight hours. Just remember to close them up tight to hold in the trapped heat.
Reduce the Use of Fans: If you have a fan in the bathroom and kitchen; minimize its usage. It sends a lot of heat out with the undesirable odors. Run them a few minutes if needed, but turn them off.
Replace Filters Often: Whether you are renting or buying your home, it's important to keep the filters in your home clean. A dirty filter in your furnace or heat pump can make the numbers rise quickly on your power bill. Swipe or replace the filters in your fans once each month. You may also have a filter in your bathroom fan, but always check to make sure it is clean, so the air remains healthy.
Crank Up the Ceiling Fans & Lower the Thermostat: Always remember that hot air rises. If you have your fan running in reverse mode, the heat will return to the floor level. Bump the thermostat down a couple of degrees. The cooler air will make a significant difference in your monthly bill. You will also sleep better, and save money (no sacrifice there).

Clear the Vents: Make sure your vents are clean so they can deliver all of the heat you are paying for every month. Be sure all of the furniture is away from the vents to prevent damage and sent you the warm air.
Use the Fireplace: You can enjoy your fireplace as you save on your minimalistic budget. Enjoy the fire, but remember to close the damper when it is not being used.

Air Conditioning
Your air conditioner can run the bill up in no time. These are just a few things you can do to help keep the power company from ruining your minimalist budget:
The Dryer: Wait until it's dark outside to run the dryer, dishwasher, and any other heat-producing appliances. Line dry your clothes instead.
The Curtains: Keep the blinds and curtains closed during the hottest part of the day.
Insulate Ductwork: Whether you rent or own your home, it is important to fully insulate the crawl spaces, garages, attics, and any other areas where air conditioning is used.
The Thermostat: Install a programmable thermostat and set it to reset the temperature when you are not at home.
If you are still having issues with your utility bill, it may be time to call the company and ask for a checkup. Many times, the visit is free or a minimal fee. The report will show you how to put the pennies back into your savings, and not to the power company.

The Water Bill
Your budget can be greatly affected by your water usage unless you take a few precautions. Consider these ways:
1. Invest in low-flow showers and toilets. The initial cost would be something you could use your savings for that would be meeting your needs.
2. As the season's change, inspect all of your fixtures and pipes in and around your home. Even a minimal leak can raise your water bill and possibly cause damage to your home.

A dripping faucet and leaky pipes are necessary expenses.

Ways to Maintain a Budget as a Minimalist
Reset the Goals
Figure out your priorities and where you went wrong with the original plan. Look out for your short and long-term goals, including buying a car, purchasing a new home, retirement, emergency savings, and don't forget that big vacation you have not taken in several years. If you lose the original plan because you placed your ideas on a back burner, identify them, and get going to reach them. Start with these options:
Emergency Savings: Make this a priority. Consider saving up enough money to cover at least three months' worth of your expenses. No matter

what the original goal was, be stricter this round. Be prepared if you have an emergency or lose your job.
Purchasing a Home or Vehicle: This goal may take a little longer. It could be four or five years away, but it is time to save the money, NOW, before your current car dies. Prepare for the unexpected as you begin your new round of minimalist living.
Remove the Debt: This is the hardest one, but it is important to become financially successful. You have to squash the debt.

Start over with a fresh budget and be sure to include these areas as a priority. Setting goals begins with a good budget.

Know How Much You 'Should Be Spending'

Live within your means! This is probably a statement you have heard many times, but it is imperative for you to achieve your goals. Once again, this cannot be stressed enough, understand where your money is going. This is the only way to keep your budget functional. There are no written rules on how to do this, but these guidelines will help you recreate and maintain a budget so you can easily reach your goals.
Break down the spending into these three main categories: financial goals, fixed costs, and flexible spending.
Fixed Costs: These are the bills that you pay monthly:
- Utilities
- Housing
- Insurance
- Cell Phone
- Legal Obligations – car payments, student loans, debt payments, etc.

Financial Goals: Whether you are saving for a home, car, or just paying off other debts, if you do not make these a part of the monthly bills, you will probably be lacking the money by the end of the month. You have to stay on top of your finances.
For example, if you have a card which carries a higher interest rate, that is a priority. If you have more than one card, pay them off according to those rates. Don't close the account, but move onto the next one and continue until they are all paid using their minimum balances (on the budget).
Flexible Spending: This category includes expenses that vary from month to month. You want to keep these in check, which includes entertainment, groceries, and dining out. Reduce the amount of money spent on food by eating at home or even inviting friends and family over for a nice dinner party.

Know What Money is Coming in and Going out
Once you know how much you *should* be spending on your budget, it is imperative that you know *where* it is all going. This basic guideline will help you identify which expenses need to be reduced.

Your Paycheck: The figure you will be looking at is your gross income/pay and is the total before any deductions, including your taxes. The net income is your take-home pay. These are the deductions that are taken:
- Social Security Taxes
- Medicare Taxes
- State Income Taxes (depending on your locality)
- Federal Income Taxes

You may also have these deductions taken from your check (so you don't have the extra paperwork):

Retirement Savings: This category is where your employer's 401(k) plan for retirement is deducted. When you sign up for the plan, you will choose a percentage to be contributed. If your employer pays into this account, try to match the amount. If you deduct 6% of your pre-taxed salary, your employer might match it with 3% (which is free money to you). At any rate, the money will add up quickly.

Insurance Payments: If you signed up with your employer for these benefits, the money would automatically come out of your check. This is just one more way to eliminate the headache of paying another bill on a scheduled date. This is a stress-free way to do this one, and you know the premium is paid promptly!

Flexible Spending (FSA) and Health Savings Accounts (HAS): These plans are used for various medical expenses (including prescriptions, co-payments, and other costs). These options are an option during open enrollment.

These are some of the ways to use these features:
- Acupuncture
- Contact lenses or prescription eyeglasses
- Laser eye surgery (LASIK)
- Chiropractic services
- Hearing Aids (repair and batteries included)
- Medications/drugs
- Insurance premiums not paid by your employer
- Smoking cessation programs
- Pregnancy test kits

These are expenses that would be difficult to pay if you don't have a plan in advance. Be sure to ask your employer for an itemized statement of your withdrawals, so you know what to expect in your paycheck. You should be able to get the information online.

Overhaul Your Spending Habits & Reward Yourself

The minimalist budget will enable you to live simple, but the process can seem endless. By calming the atmosphere and emotions, your desires will also dwindle. Try to remember, you cannot have it all, and more is less. Maintaining a minimalist budget is hard work. Therefore, recall the old saying, "All work and no play makes Jack a dull boy." As a child, you have probably heard it many times, and it's still true as an adult. You have worked hard to achieve your status. After all, acquiring the discipline and preparation for achieving your goals is difficult, to say the least.

When you meet a goal, have a special dinner at your favorite restaurant or have a salon or spa treatment. Plan ahead, so you have an extra incentive to reach - once your budgeting milestone has been achieved.

Move on and raise the bar, but always look forward to your accomplishments.

"You have succeeded in life when all you really want is only what you really need." —Vernon Howard

Chapter 8: Reorganize The Bedrooms

If you are like many people, your bedroom seems to be the storage space whenever it is clean-up time. If so, you already understand that you have your work cut out without a game plan. Get out the boxes and begin your routine.

The best plan includes removing all items from under the bed (dust bunnies included). Ideally, under the bed storage is good for those who are limited to space, but we tend to forget what is under the lurking space! Strip and clean the curtains to refresh the room. If you are considering a remodel, have a new pattern ready to hang with your nicely cleaned area. Choose a color scheme and stick with it. Your tidy home appearance will be beautiful.

The Bed

Strip the bed down to the mattress. It is essential to vacuum the mattress and bed springs to remove the dead skin (yuck), dust, and dust mites. Be sure to vacuum the perimeter of the bed, which is a haven for mites. Remove all of the bed linens and wash them. Pillowcases should be done weekly, and the bed protectors should be washed monthly. For blankets, decide whether it is washable or dry clean only. If it is clean, just fold and go. Most pillows are machine washable—and should be washed seasonally to remove any lingering odors, stains, mold, or bacteria.

Purchase an under-the-bed drawer for optimizing your spaces. Label the container so that you are always aware of its contents.

Prepare this aroma for the room:

Healthy Bedtime Spray for the Monsters

Even though this is not a spray you use on your body; it classifies a spot in the bedtime aroma section. Some customers have called it the 'Shoo the Monsters Away' spray remedy.

Try this blend using the specified amount of drops:
- Emulsifier - 30
- Orange - 8
- Lavender 12
- Roman Chamomile -2
- 8-ounce bottle of room spray base

How to Mix:
1. Mix the oils with the emulsifier and base. Shake well.

How to Use:
1. Simply spray the monsters away and freshen the room.
2. Spray a bit on the pillow for extra pleasure.

The Dresser

It is best to remove all distractions from the surfaces in the bedroom except for special items or items which require daily access. A few pictures and knick-knacks are acceptable as long as you don't have a resulting clutter zone. Many of the famous designers recommend a compartmentalized wooden box on top of the dresser. It will contain all of the daily items such as eyeglasses, remotes, phones, and similar objects. Everything is corralled into one neat space.

Bedside Tables

Your bedside table is another good hiding place for items when you don't want to do any chores. Take a box with you for the keep-trash-donate items. It is much simpler if you keep all of the items together, so later; you won't be tempted to rummage through the boxes (via packrat time).

Make a future plan for the drawers with drawer organizers. You can easily see what you want without destroying the room to locate the desired item.

The Book Clutter

If your bedside table ends up looking like a bookstore, it might be advisable to purchase a nightstand that has shelves. As you work, discard the books that you have already read. Only leave your current reading material or other essential items on the tabletop.

If you have a hobby such as needlepoint or knitting; use an under the bed storage container for the items. You can also place an attractive bench or cedar chest at the foot of the bed for hiding some items.

Ladies & Your Makeup

As with medicines you should not store your makeup in the bathroom. Find a spot somewhere in the bedroom to store your precious cosmetics and other similar products.

Check all of your products for expiration dates, such as sunscreen or lotion. If it is not the same consistency that it was when it was purchased and didn't have a date marked, it has probably lost its beneficial qualities. In other words, it's trash.

Go through hair products and personal care items. If the product has a unique smell, it is probably trash! These are some guidelines for your makeup:

- *Eyeliner Products:* Gel eyeliner lasts approximately six to eight months because of the double-dipping of a brush into a pot. However, a pencil is good for one year. According to sources at the *Huffington Post*, sharpening a pencil is not going to be a bacterial breeding ground, so don't worry.
- *Eye Shadow and Other Powder Cosmetics:* Powder products do last longer than wet formulas. Most products are good from one to two years. As with other products, it is smells, toss it!

- *Lipstick:* Expiration will be shown by texture, smell, or color changes. If you wipe/clean them off with a bit of alcohol, they will remain sanitized.
- *Foundation:* Packaged foundation in a pot usually lasts about six months, but a pump formula can last for one or two years.
- *Any Natural Products:* Consider keeping preservative-free/natural cosmetics in the refrigerator. The shelf life of many is approximately three to six months. However, check with the manufacturing company.

Jewelry

The jewelry is an area that may take a bit more time. Do that on your 'special' day set aside for special projects. You can do this action when you have some quality time to reflect and make the necessary decisions whether the item should be in the keep-toss-donate-or gift box. However, you can clean the outside of the box.

The Closet

The closet is another forbidden territory because you just know you don't want to throw any of your favorite items away. Look at the brighter side; if you haven't worn the item within the past year, it is time to bid the item a fond farewell.

Begin by letting go of the guilt of how many times you have left it hanging in the closet. If the garment or article has collected dust, it's definitely time to hit-the-road.

Maintain Dirty Laundry: Designate a spot in the closet or a hidden corner for dirty clothes until laundry day. Be sure all of the items are dry before you stow them away or you could have moldy clothing. Ideally, take them to the laundry room if space permits. Another option is to purchase an over-the-door hamper if you don't have the extra floor space.

Purchase Closet Rod Expanders: You can utilize your closet space by adding an extension rod to make the space efficient. You can create sections for hanging blouses and pants without the lost space between them and your shoes.

Use Shelf Dividers: It might seem a bit fussy, but shelf dividers are the answer to organizing any space. First, you need to count how many divided stacks you will need, whether it is for shirts, jeans, or sweaters. You can also use these dividers in the bathroom or any area that can benefit from them because they hook/slip over any solid shelf.

Measure the width and height between the shelf the ceiling or next highest shelf. You can choose from different styles such as white, wire, chrome, and many others. Tall solid dividers are excellent for storing handbags.

You can use a bookshelf with deep shelves for sweaters, tee-shirts, sweats, shorts, jogging pants, and similar clothing.

Roll the Clothes: Professional organizers have discovered you can get approximately 1/3 more shirts in a drawer using the fold-and-roll technique. This presents a huge advantage because you can see which shirt you are searching for because it is rolled and not folded flat.

Fold the shirt in approximately 4 inches from the bottom. Fold in one side of the shirt with the sleeve out, and repeat on the other side.

Roll the shirt from the collar downwards. You should be able to see the pattern on the shirt with this roll. This particular type of roll is similar to the military technique, but it is not as tightly gathered.

How to Hang Clothing:
- Similar colors together
- Hang the sweaters together
- Shirts together
- Pants and skirts together
- Dresses together

Purchase a batch of velvet hangers for the flimsy items that won't otherwise stay on the hangers. Remove the empty hangers to the laundry room. Don't leave a tangled mess on the floor or occupying precious hanging spaces. Besides, it looks messy.

Classify the Clothes:

With so many decisions, here is a way to categorize the items easily:
- **Keep Box:** Clothes you will wear for the next year, clothes that look good, and clothes that fit good
- **Cosign Box**: Clothes you no longer need which are in excellent condition
- **Donate Box**: All clothes in good condition
- **Trash**: Throw out the unusable (stained, torn, minus buttons) garments or reuse the material for another project.

Major Tip: Keep in mind; don't hoard it unless you have a plan, or you will end up with another messy disaster.

The Shoe Section

Place all of your shoes in a line and separate them into categories, for work or dress wear. Decide whether you wear them or if they need to be tossed or donated. If you haven't worn them in the last few months, get rid of them. However, don't throw away any seasonal items such as rain boots or winter gear.

You can purchase a sectional cubby that can be used as one unit to store your shoes and handbags. It will keep them off the floor and readily available when you are ready to use them.

The Scarves, Hats, and Purses

Scarves, belts, purses, and other accessories also need to go through the decision-making process. Purchase an accessory organization tool that will hold ten to twelve scarves on one hanger. They can also hang on a regular hanger in the closet.

If you have a lot of hats, you can purchase a hanger that used clips to store them. You can also roll the belts and ties and place them neatly in a dresser drawer.

Ways to Minimalize Your Clothing Between Seasons

Keeping your wardrobe appealing to the eye is all a part of minimalistic living. You can see your clothes and won't be concentrated on going shopping. The process involves creating what is called a clothing capsule. The process of getting dressed will be much easier when you know where to look. Use some of the suggestions and make your own capsule rules and guidelines. Just remember, keep it simple; if you don't absolutely love it; chuck it in the trash or donate box.

Benefits of a Clothing Capsule

You will be surprised how many benefits you will receive from taking the extra effort to prepare a clothing capsule. These are just a few:

- You will be enjoying the newly created closet space. It is so organized (making it easier to remain that way). You will be spending less money and time purchasing new clothes because you commit to owning fewer pieces you truly love.
- Your confidence will be boosted since you now realize every item in the space looks great on you in a flattering way!
- You can leisurely prepare for an outing or work. You know where all of your essential and fancier items are stored.
- The stress factor will be removed. You will no longer have that overwhelming feeling of fatigue of what to wear!
- You will feel and be grateful and content with what you have, instead of concentrating on your next shopping spree!

In a nutshell, you'll be spending less energy and time when you're getting dressed. You will discover the kept items make you look and feel great.

You spend less energy and time getting dressed. Everything in your wardrobe feels and looks superb on you. Less time and energy is focused on your clothes, which means more time and energy are focused on you.

Begin Your Capsule

Make yourself set limitations on the number of items you add to the capsule. Don't stress out for a set 33 items you will read about in the next segment, but be reasonable and sort the items you will wear and see where it takes you. Include only items in the capsule that are worn daily.

What not to include in the capsule:
- Jewelry & Accessories: Earrings, necklaces, bracelets, scarves, etc.
- Outerwear: Hats, Jackets, gloves, etc.
- Shoes: Casual, formal, and business

- Workout clothes: Sweatpants, leggings, etc.
- Undergarments: Socks, underwear, bras, and tank tops or camisoles
- Seasonal personal gear and swimwear
- Formal Clothing: Fancy skirts, business clothes, dresses, skirts, and similar items)

Decide on a Timeframe

Most people will switch the capsule every three months or at least when the seasons change. Store all of the capsule items in the closet of the items you are currently wearing. Store the off-season items in spare closets or dressers. Remember, simple, and clutter-free is the answer to serenity.

CHAPTER 9
For Kids Only — Minimalism

Children's clothing will require more persistence since he/she grows in spurts and go through more clothing. Use the same logic used in your closet.

Manage the Clothing

Make the sorting process much simpler by expanding your keep box; place the items being worn now in a box (or use the bed). Sort the clothes that are out-of-season in another section. After you finish sorting the articles, place them neatly into the dresser.

Remove the donate box outside of the room in case you need to make more space.

Project 333 Rules - How to Manage Children's Clothes

The 333 project is one of the most popular minimalist challenges that will invite you to dress your child with 33 items or less for three months. You can begin the process at any time, but it is sometimes a good idea to initiate the time during the months of October 1 until December 31 or another time of the year when your schedule is less busy.

- *Items to Keep*: The items you will use as the 33 items include outerwear, shoes, clothing, jewelry (if the child has any), and accessories.

- *Items Not Included*: You would not count underwear and pajamas.

- *Make a List*: About two months before you begin the purge, make an outline of the items you will keep. At the end of that time, box up the remainder of the items and place them in a box. Tape the box closed and put it out of sight. (Remember this later. If you have not needed the items, the professionals suggest donating the box without looking at the contents.)

- *Which Items to Remove:* Consider the items that will be most used. If you purchase new items for Project 333, use the one in and two out approach, but always stick to no more than the 33 items.

- *Sentimental Items:* Choose a drawer/shelf/container to hold on to sentimental things like the first outfit, first shoes, etc. Once again, be ruthless, and keep only a handful of pieces of clothing that your child really loved.

Ways to Make the Created Wardrobe Functional

Choose a cohesive style and color palette. You need to be able to mix and match your clothing, so you don't need enormous amounts of extra pieces to put an outfit together. Owning fewer items make getting ready for the day a much simpler task.

Decide when enough is enough. You can provide a seasonal capsule until each of the items it is totally functional. Once you have the items of clothing sorted with usable items that you must have, set the options in the same pod and close them for the year.

Bear in mind, to keep items that can be used for all times of the year in a space that is easily accessible. By reducing the clutter, you can quickly discover a jacket or swimsuit as the season permits without destroying the cleaned closet.

By making a capsule wardrobe, the collection of clothing will consist of items that are worn regularly and can be interchanged. Figure out exactly how many socks, bottoms, tops, and outerwear your child can go through weekly. If you are not sure what that amount will be, consider placing a laundry basket aside for nothing but his/her clothing.

For older children, you might consider this experiment a bit longer since they tend to be more fashion conscious. Add another three to five days of clothing for the calculations.

Be brutal with the choices and discard anything that is stained too small or big—or items that are not worn. Use the same keep, toss, and donate boxes as used with the toys. If you have more than one child, you need to consider not saving so many items for the next child. By the time the second child needs the item, it could be out of season or completely out of style. Don't use valuable space for storing questionable items.

By following these guidelines, you will discover there will not be any more digging for items that do not work well together. You will have clothing that can be coordinated with other items without worrying about whether they match. This learning process provides your child with a way of learning independence when he/she can choose what to wear.

About the Toys

Does your home seem like everywhere you look—you have an unending supply of toys? How many should you keep? What will you do with them? The answers are fairly simple, with a bit of practice.

Observe which toys they play with the most, keep the ones that can fit on the shelves, keep the ones that encourage creativity, and encourage them to donate ones they don't play with often to kids in need.

Keep in mind that toys can be educational and can play an essential role in his/her development. Those are the types of toys you will want to have in your home. Once you have these questions, it's time to proceed with how to eliminate the clutter.

Fads and Trendy Toys
Be firm and don't give in to all of the advertisements you see broadcasted. Companies will generate new toys every few months and plaster them over every television network that is available. Your child sees the toy as an item that must belong in his/her toy-box. Children are viewing these advertisements and do not understand why the room cannot be filled up with each of these new items. You have to draw the line and say no if the room is already at its maximum capacity.

Don't feel alone because every parent goes through this. The fad will pass, but maybe it is time for some commercial-free entertainment. So, just keep a realistic and healthy attitude toward the toy manufacturers and realize which ones will be educational and which ones are out there to make money for the businesses selling the 'trendy' products.

Limit Shopping Adventures
Have you ever been in a store and experience a temper tantrum because a child did not get a 'must have' toy? If it happens to you, you have to remain firm so your youngster won't believe throwing a fit will get him/her a new toy. By not giving in to the tantrum, you are teaching limitations. Don't worry about what others may think because you know your situation, and they don't!

Rent Toys & Save Space
Check in your area to locate a <u>toy library</u>. Consider borrowing toys instead of purchasing them. Check the extensive list to see if there is one in your area of the United States. Your children can enjoy the toy, but you can always return it instead of worrying about how to pay for it.

Beginning the Process
Plan ahead when it is a time of approaching events in the child's life, such as a birthday or holiday that will be adding more toys to the cleared space. Help your child understand you need to make room for additional toys. If you begin the process when the child is young, it will be a permanent thought pattern for the future.

Keeping the Organization
Some older children like to see the belongings on a higher closet shelf. Clear plastic containers are good for storing smaller pieces so you can quickly identify the contents. It will eliminate a lot of unnecessary searching and digging for a special something (we all do it).

Keep the clutter controlled by bargaining. Tell the child that he/she can have the Lego set once the trucks are securely parked in the correct spaces. *Make the items simpler to put away than they were to retrieve.* Think of the space from a child's perspective; the floor is his/her table. If you place the flip-file picture books upright in a plastic dishpan or similar container, your kid has to rummage through the stack to find the desired one. The unwanted ones will be on the floor but consider the alternative. Compare a normal/traditional bookcase where the tiny fingers can wipe out the entire shelf with one swipe. You should see the picture now!

Organize using the bottom to top method. The children's most used items should be located on the lower shelves and drawers or left on the floor. Designate the higher levels for the items which are seldom used. For example, the breakable bear collection is eight-feet off of the floor, whereas the favorite bear is awaiting company in the rocking chair.

Label Everything

If you have a toddler, use a computer printer to make some simple but graphic labels for the clothing articles. For example, use a picture of shirts, socks, dolls, trucks, or any other item that might remind your kid of where the item lives! Good luck with that one!

Put labels in the closets, inside of the drawers, on the edges of shelves, the plastic bins—everywhere. Make it a game and play 'match the label.' It can be a lot of fun, and the child is learning how to become organized.

CHAPTER 10
Declutter Laundry Spaces

Replace the Items in the Laundry Room
The Cabinets: Group all of the similar products, such as laundry detergent, bleach, and fabric sheets. Be sure you have some all-purpose cleaners available for quick cleanups.

Add some baskets or plastic containers to the tops of the washer and dryer for your convenience. Place one box for the clothes hangers or neatly hang them on a laundry rack if you have one.

Purchase some stackable plastic, wicker, or similar style decorative boxes for sorting the laundry. When you are in a time crunch, or any other time, you can use the smaller baskets for sorting the socks and undies that take so much time to pair and fold. Empty or full, the area is organized!

Sorted Laundry: If you have the extra space in the laundry room; place some sorter baskets in the area to keep dirty laundry organized. You can purchase the sorters reasonably priced, so as each piece of laundry can be added to its designated section as it becomes dirty, instead of the heaps of unsorted disasters that can happen. The canvas styles are very attractive and forgiving if you accidentally place a damp article in the hamper.

Note: Try to be sure all items are completely dry before you place them in the laundry hamper. The dampness could promote mildew on the clothing or other articles.

CHAPTER 11
Clean & Organize Spare Storage Areas

You have put off the least used rooms until last during your normal cleaning routines. It is time to tackle those junk collection havens to remove items you either don't need or don't use.

Real Simple Magazine once ran an article about a numbering system for miscellaneous articles. The plan is unique and can use your imagination in the process of design. It will work especially well for sewing or craft projects.

Choose some decorative boxes that are all the same sizes. Place fancy numbers on the outside end of each one and store them neatly on a shelf. Keep a catalog of what items are placed in the box. When you need something and have no clue where it's at; simply look at the catalog.

The Basement

The basement must also follow the keep-toss-donate-trash boxes. The basement in many homes is the graveyard for many 'you are going to fix it' items. As you begin the chore in the basement, think of how long the item has already been waiting. For example, you put that pair of shoes on the shelf; umm, no answer, huh? So many items are waiting for the trash pile. This is a molehill that has now become a mountain.

The Attic

The attic is another great spot for storing hidden treasures. If you store our seasonal items in the attic, you should sort through them the same way you did in the bedroom closet. Purchase a hanging caddy/rack for coats and similar items to conserve space. Be sure to have the keep-toss-donate-trash bins close at hand.

Seasonal Decorations: If you like to decorate with changes of the seasons, you need to figure out a way to keep them all separated. Use different colored/types of bins to distinguish what season the box is for, and label the outside of the container showing its contents clearly—no more digging. The Christmas decorations have a way of becoming disorganized. Purchase some plastic bins which are available to store everything from wrapping paper to your most fragile ornaments. Not only will you be thankful when you can locate the items, but you will also be saving spaces for other essential household items.

The Luggage: How many pieces of luggage does your family need? Be honest and keep the ones you use and donate the rest of the lot. Another useful tip, just in case you cannot part with the extra pieces, use them for storage—place off-season gear in them. Winter blankets can go in them during the summer months. The ideas are limitless, especially if you live in a crowded home. Make the extra pieces worth the space you are using.

The Garage

Broken furniture seems to collect in the garage. The items come along with explanations of; it only needs a screw, or I can cover that. Unfortunately, the items have started a party in the garage with chairs and tables on the guest list! What happened to the space you had for two cars? It is time to fix it or toss it.

Plan on going through all of the boxes to discover how many items can go to donate/toss stack, especially the ones already destined to be yard sale or thrift store material.

If you have cabinets and drawers, go through each of them. For small items such as screws, nuts, and bolts can be stored in baby food jars or other types of containers for storage organization. (You might need to choose day 11 after the plan).

After you finish sorting the boxes and other spaces, be sure to mark the boxes for its contents clearly. It is a good idea to date the box so that you will remember when it was last purged.

The Garage Refrigerator or Freezer: Remove everything from the refrigerator or freezer and thoroughly clean it, just as you did the one inside of the home. It is a good idea to check the contents of the unit, especially if you have stored a lot of meat or veggies in the freezer.

Note: If you are a hunter, consider donating or selling any leftover game meat to hunters in your area. Many of the clubs will use it to feed the dogs (even freezer burnt meat). It is better than throwing it into the garbage.

Sports Gear: Consolidate your gear into categories, making sure all of the camping gear is in one place, and the tennis or golf equipment is safely stored in another. Look over the equipment and discard any damaged items. Use your imagination and hang some of the items until the season changes and you need it again.

Hang the Tools: Consider putting pegboards on the wall so you can find the hammer or screwdriver the next time it is needed. Hang the yard or garden tools such as the hoe, shovel, or rake.

Use larger hooks to suspend large items such as bicycles to provide more walking space.

Plastic shelving is an excellent way to provide extra storage for smaller items. You can purchase the units that reach the ceiling for additional spaces for any items. Just be sure not to overload it. Check the weight limits when you make a purchase from a home improvement store, supercenter, or second-hand store.

Downsize your car if possible. Do you really need a 4x4 when a compact model would serve your needs? Think of the money saved that could be applied to other essential items in your budget.

Your Vehicle Needs a Cleaning Also: Make a new daily habit when you get home from work or other outings. Remove all of the trash and other items that don't live in the car.

CHAPTER 12
Methods Of Containment & Removal

"It is always the simple that produces the marvelous." —Amelia Barr
Set specific rules for kids clutter. Depending on the child's age, only allow toys in the bedroom. Designate the kitchen, dining room, and living spaces for household items only. For smaller children or toddlers, choose a space in the home, such as a corner where the toys can be neatly stored in containers, shelves, or bookcases.

Cubbies: A small plastic three-drawer organizer is an excellent choice for smaller items such as Legos, blocks, or stuffed animals. Remember to keep the most cherished ones.

Bins and Baskets: These are a safe and easy way to make clean up simpler. Label each of the bins if possible so that you and your child (age dependent) will know the correct location of each article. If your child has not reached the age to associate with reading yet, you can use some pictures for the label.

A Home for Similar Items: If possible, keep all of the stuffed animals, sports items, and other special items in the same container or space. Use the same logic with socks, underwear, pants, shirts, shorts, and other foldable items.

School Papers: It is essential to have a special location for school papers. Many schools use the phone system for relaying messages, which helps eliminate a lot of the paper clutter. However, there are many other papers that need to be filed. Use an inbox or folder system for incoming paperwork. Take advantage of the Google Calendar and enter the information on it as soon as you receive notification of any upcoming events.

Now that you have the items secured in special places, it's time to decide what to do with the items you have decided have cluttered your living space. The next step is to decide where the designated boxes you have to 'sell' and 'donate' will be placed. It's much easier than it sounds.

Removal of Clutter

Visit a local consignment store in your area. You can also sell items of value on Craigslist or eBay to make money from the items you've decided you don't need. Try local selling apps to make a quick and easy sale. All you need is a photo, a short description, and a price. Some of these apps will allow payments inside of the app.

1. *OfferUp:* You can take one to four photos and enter the title of the article you will be selling. Add the condition and set a price. You can also share your item to Facebook. You will receive a notification to let you know when someone wants your item. You get paid from the interested buyer once you choose a safe area to meet.

2. *5miles:* This tremendous local selling app requires at least one photo (add more if needed), and add it to the correct selling category. You can also upload a video. Post your location, a description, and price for the item. Post it on Twitter or Facebook for additional advertising. The app goes beyond others and allows users to list local services, jobs, housing, and a list of yard sales. You can choose to be paid through the 5miles by using their credit or debit card or handle it by cash, the old-fashioned way.
3. *LetGo:* This is a favorite app since it can have your item up for sale in less than one minute. You can change your price and location or share the article you would like to sell and share it on Facebook. You will be contacted through the app for questions. You will have to handle the transaction made through the app, which is about the only downfall.
4. *Shpock*: This site offers an easy listing for your information. All you need to do is choose a category, provide a title, description, and price. Share on Facebook. The app is free, but premium membership is offered, which will remove the additional ads. You can add more photos and have the ability to move your listings to the top of the search result list.
5. *Trove:* As you are downsizing, consider using this site to sell your furniture. You can also purchase items! Choose a category, take a photo, and add the title with its details. The list is easy to list the condition, brand, width, depth, and height. You will need to sign into Facebook or Google to complete your listing.
6. *VarageSale:* Take a few minutes to add a title, category, price, and description of your item. To activate the account will require a Facebook login. The administration will verify your profile photo and real name before you are activated.
7. *Close5:* This app was created by eBay so you can sell your belongings in your locality. All you do is decide on a location, price, and description. Share your listing on Facebook. Set a 'Best Offer' for the item which allows the client to make the offer (less stressful for you). It is your emergency fund, so choose wisely.

Check These Resources

- *Staples and Office Depot*: These two companies will take your empty ink and toner cartridges. You can earn rewards which you can use in turn to purchase other essential items to suit your budget.

- *Best Buy*: You can receive a Best Buy gift card either online or in the store. All you need are old electronics such as computers, tablets, cell phones, GPS units, and many other items you may otherwise throw in the trash.

Purchase essential items in Bulk: Sam's Club is one of the most well-known choices, but check your area for other places. At any rate, if you have enough savings in your budget, it is worthwhile to purchase items when they are on sale.

Sell Jewelry: If you have jewelry that is collecting dust in your jewelry box, consider selling it online or at a pawn shop. You may be surprised how much extra money you can add to your budget with items you never wear. Each of these methods will allow you to recover some of the losses as you begin your minimalistic journey. It can also be a good starting point for your emergency funds. You will receive money for items you no longer need and still be formatting a baseline for your savings.

CHAPTER 13
Benefits Of A Minimalistic Home

"Truth is ever to be found in simplicity, and not in the multiplicity and confusion of things." —Isaac Newton

More Focus on Fun and Healthier Activities
Remove material possessions out of your life that can cause you extra work. Think of the time spent on a dune buggy that goes out only during the summer months. Take the extra time to go for a hike or to go fishing or hunting with friends. Do what you can to enjoy yourself anytime, whether it is playing with your kids or family members out in the yard picking a guitar. Have fun and enjoy life.
Once you have your budget in a workable manner, you will have more confidence and have time to enjoy life. You have removed the worry and stress, which can be linked to depression.

Focus Less on Material Belongings
Once you have gained the freedom from materialism, you will begin to think with a changed mindset. Once you have decluttered your living spaces, basement, and garage; you will discover how many things are just not needed in your life.
Think of the boat you have the garage that you only take out once or twice a year. You can - not only lower payments (unless it is paid for) - but think of the space where you could do other things. Have a party and celebrate the removal of unnecessary items. But, don't forget that the bulk of the sale should be added into your emergency fund account.

You Are Given the Freedom to Spend Your Money
You can ask anyone that has maintained a minimalist budget, and one out of ten will answer that the philosophy of freedom on the top of the list. Don't let that idea get too far ahead of the plan. When you begin to spend money on things that are important to you; you will start to minimize your spending. You will discover that buying it because it is on sale is not a good reason. Are you buying it because your neighbor has one? If the answer is yes; think about the pending purchase. Do you really need or want the item?

Appreciate Your Belongings
Once you have your budget plan in action and understand the differences between your wants and needs, the process will be much easier to accomplish. You will discover that you can fulfill your desires quicker than you realized. That is the turning point you are seeking in your minimalist budget.

There will always be something you 'want,' but as a minimalist, you will realize you cannot currently afford the item or service. The focus is clearer once your expenditures have been documented. Don't think of it as being deprived, because you really aren't. Think of the many ways you are blessed.

This is the viewpoint held by an individual who is a minimalist. You can decide what is important to you and your family. Now, go for it! It may take more time, but you will not be deeper in debt. That alone is worth the waiting time. You are empowered and capable – not deprived.

You'll Have Healthier Relationships

As a human being, everyone needs to connect with other humans. A minimalistic lifestyle and home will help you put a focus on people instead of the stuff they have. There's just more room and space and more energy for people in relationships to flourish. You cannot build a satisfying connection around possessions, not even shared possessions. Minimalism is making a conscious choice to use the things and people we love because the opposite will not bring you the connections for very long.

You Stress Less About Finances

The minimalist approach will free up your valuable resources of energy and time as well as money. When you become disengaged with being like all of your neighbors, everything else comes naturally. You have built your life on money, and so many times, you have found herself discontent. You need to tune out all of the commercials trying to say you can purchase at a special price, and devote your time to other things. Minimalism is a path to get out of debt. There isn't any need to spend money on items to impress people around you.

All you're doing is giving up items you don't need, so many of which would need maintenance as time passes.

Cleaning Is Easier

If you're like many people, you want to enjoy a clean house, but you hate doing housework. A minimalistic way of living will provide you with this incentive, so you're more likely to get it done and stay on top of the housework. For example, if you have to pick up, dust off, and deal with ten items on the countertop, it just takes too much effort after a long day! Multiply that by how many rooms you have cluttered. On the minimalist side of things, just move a few items, vacuum, and maybe pick up a couple of misplaced items. You are much more likely to get the vacuuming done.

Happiness Is Less Cleaning

Once you have fully cleaned and organized your spaces, you can simply do a quick clean/pick up of any misplaced items on the way to your bedroom before retiring for the evening. There's no reason or need to wake up in the morning to a cluttered mess. After you realize how easy it is to maintain a tidy and clean home, you will discover it is a great benefit to minimalism.

Minimalism Helps You Thrive as a Highly Sensitive Person

If you are in this category and also an introvert, minimalism is your friend. Because of this, having a calm and uncluttered home is important. Too much visual clutter or a chaotic environment can cause the feeling of being stressed and overwhelmed.

If you want your home to be your sanctuary, as a place where you can feel peaceful, calm, and recharged; minimalist living is for you. Learning how much an uncluttered, minimalist home and life would benefit you as a highly sensitive person is empowering and motivating.

You'll Cultivate Gratitude

Harvard Medical School defines gratitude as "a thankful appreciation for what an individual receives, whether tangible or intangible." Studies show that people who feel more gratitude tend to be happier, more optimistic, and feel better about their lives. You break the cycle of thinking if you just have the latest gadgets or the newest styles of clothes or the trendiest furniture; you will then finally be happy. You are choosing to feel grateful and happy for what you already have.

When you actively seek the good things in life, then appreciate the good things around you and feel grateful for them. When you come from a place of gratitude and contentment, you aren't searching for happiness in things you can buy. You look for happiness inside yourself. And in your fulfilling relationships, in the ways you spend your time that bring you joy, etc.

True happiness comes from within your heart when you notice and appreciate all the good things in your life; both tangible and intangible. True happiness comes when you actively look for a reason to *feel* happy and grateful—even in the times when that's hard to do.

Benefits of the Minimalist Budget Plan

Commit to your new way of life with your minimalist budget plan with the following benefits:

Priorities are redirected: You can see just what you and your family are spending. You have a blueprint each month to make the goals easier to obtain.

Waste is revealed. As you live day-to-day, life can become hectic. Unless you have a budget, you can get lost in all of the wasted time and money.

Stress is reduced. Many times, your financial standing is the leader of stress. You have a sense of control of your money - as it comes and goes out once you have a plan. You can feel more empowered with the ease of making your budget and sticking with the plan.

New habits are created. Once you realize that life is too short to stress over the old habits of spending money, you will have a minimalist budget. Once you have a clear picture of how to keep track of your income and expenses, you will be more conscious of spending your money unnecessarily.

Set the goals. Set those goal lines high, but not so high that you cannot do the climb. Once you have all of the facts noted using whatever method of organization you use, your life will be happier for you and your family. How much more can you ask of motivation?

Stay educated. You can view your money as a tool as you shift your mindset to focus on your future needs and your long-term goals. It is great to make those, but it is also essential to remain 'on task' and keep up with the times.

Improved motivation is evident. Creating and staying motivated with your new budget can be exhausting and mentally taxing until you have all of the figures in the right column. However, keep in mind that motivation is the first step, but you have to continue all the way through the process. Start one month at a time until you have it right. You will be glad when you can have a nice 'nest egg' for the 'rainy days' of your future.

You can be yourself. Always embrace your situation and don't think of your budget as a chore. It is the key to your financial success. Learning how to live on the minimalist budget may be contagious.

Make space in your life. Downsize your life, and you will be surprised how much money can be saved. Remember two things; follow the budget, and be frugal. You will begin to think about each purchase and how much it can or cannot fit in your simplified budget plan.

Change is good. Be ready to make huge changes in your life. Learning how to live with less is truly a blessing in disguise. You may be thinking that all you are doing is throwing away your stuff. In essence, you are doing much more than that. You are removing all of the waste that has taken over your life. By removing your paper clutter in the process, you are uncovering new ways to save money. By maintaining your budget regularly, you and your family are ensured that if an emergency should arise, you will be ready to face it.

You are not only growing financially, but you are learning how success really does feel! You sincerely have your minimalist mindset in gear. You are now preparing for your family's future and well-being.

CHAPTER 14
The Minimalist Mindset

"Purity and simplicity are the two wings with which man soars above the earth and all temporary nature." —Thomas Kempis

Minimalistic thinking allows you to become a gatekeeper about what's allowed in your home and in your life. You need to realize that happiness doesn't come from items. Consider the logic of why:

There's always a shiny new item right in front of you. New styles, models, features, and multiple new improvements are just around the corner. From kitchen gadgets to cars and unlimited technology, your world continues to move forward. Planned discontinuance will ensure your recent purchase will be out of use sooner; not later.

All new items will fade. By nature, all possessions are temporary. They look stunning in the store. However, think about it, as soon as the item is purchased, it will begin to age or spoil.

Possessions require maintenance. Your purchase will require focus, energy, and time for cleaning. The items can create more work since they will need to be cleaned and maintained. Many times they will become a distraction from the things that can truly bring you extended happiness.

Each purchase can add more stress to your life. For every extra physical item that you bring into your life, it will represent one more item to be scratched, stolen, or broken!

Shopping does not extinguish your oldest desire for contentment. Your overflowing closets and drawers stand as proof the purchases do not stop the drive. No matter how much you get; it's never enough.

Consider activities rather than shopping: Of course, the list can begin with decluttering a drawer or organizing your shoes, but that might not be ideal.
- Tackle a little bit of yard work and be too tired to consider the mall.
- Exercise with a friend and burn away a few pounds, besides making yourself feel great!
- Organize your photos and clean out your email files. Clear the junk out!
- Start a new novel and create a beautiful space. Create one of your own!

You will own less, not purging more: Shop more intentionally and thoughtfully. Stop buying things you do not need. Keep the standards high of all items you place in your wardrobe. If you add one, take one away, if not two to discard.

Value experiences over physical items: Millennials are prioritizing their vehicles and homes - less and less. They're enlisting more importance to personal experiences. One study found that <u>72%</u> of millennials would rather spend more money on *experiences* than on material things.

Make better use of your time; become more intentional. You can start small but start now by letting just one item leave your space. You may not make a big step every day, but you're headed in the right direction. As you minimize your clutter, you are intentionally clearing objects that keep you from happiness.

Make gradual shifts in your attitude. Each decision you make will build your confidence and head you in the right direction. Your self-confidence will also get a boost as you clear your mind and space. With each decision, the process becomes quicker and easier. You are empowered to consume less and live more!

Realize, organizing is not the only answer. If you get stuck on one item or topic, just move onto something else and regroup your thinking pattern. There will always be situations or items you will need to add more thought to before a decision can be made. The process works in stages, so move on and keep the momentum going.

Make the commitment and play games to keep the process more fun. Make a challenge to yourself and set a goal of donating an article of clothing every day for one month. At that point, take the bag to a collection center. You will not only be helping others, but you are also learning the true meaning of a minimalist. You just removed items that did not bring your joy without realizing you reached one of your goals

Stop letting others have an effect on what stays in your home. The professionals stress the best way to achieve the benefits of minimalism is to start from within yourself. Make the example that others will desire to follow. Avoid making decisions on items you share with other family members or others living in shared situations. Cross that bridge only when absolutely necessary. Let the others be involved in the decisions of his or her belongings. By all means, stop comparing yourself to what you own as to what others have.

What Children Learn as a Minimalist

- You gladly share with others.
- You don't need to live life like everyone else.
- You don't need to buy things to be happy.
- You think carefully about our purchases.
- You live within your means.
- You love spending time with them.
- We are in control of our stuff.

If your children are still very small, adopting a minimalist lifestyle will be a lot easier than if they're older and have already accumulated a lot of stuff. However, don't let that put you off. It might not be easy, and you'll probably find yourself battling some resistance, but stick with it.

CHAPTER 15
The Minimalist Plan For Home Maintenance

"In order to seek one's own direction, one must simplify the mechanics of ordinary, everyday life." —Plato

You have reached a cornerstone and now have a clean house. Your next question is how to keep it clean. You won't be considered a clean freak because it is a minimalistic home for you to be proud to enjoy with your friends and family. This simplified approach is just what you need:

The Guiding Rule: Simplify! As you have learned, it's much simpler and less stressful once you realize less is more.

- Less furniture is much easier to clean.
- Fewer clothes will mean less clothing to wash, fold, and put away. You might have plenty of clothes, but you won't have them piled high in a corner lurking.
- Less kitchen clutter means you can clean the kitchen quickly after you prepare a meal. You won't need to shuffle the unessential items on the countertops!

Meditate While You Clean: You can remove a ton of stress if you put your mind in a peaceful place. Think of yourself as a monk sweeping the floors of a temple.

Wash While You Cook: On a similar note, wash as you cook. In any downtime, be cleaning up. I like to clean everything or at least rinse everything before I sit down to eat. I basically don't have to come back and clean up later. It takes me about two minutes after I'm done eating to clean up.

Don't Forget to Clean the Windows & Blinds: Pay extra attention to these two areas, especially if you have children or pets. The dust can accumulate quickly, making it unsightly and distracting as you continue your new minimalist behaviors. The natural light provides you with minimal portions of Vitamins C and D. So, bring in all the light!

Pair Your Cleaning Tasks

You probably already pair tasks without realizing you're doing it. But I like to intentionally pair tasks to make mundane chores a little bit more purposeful. There are three parts to pairing tasks.

Phase One: While you do a chore, do something fun while you're doing it, such as listening to an audiobook while you're dusting. Look forward and learn how to associate your tasks with your favorite show. Chores do not need to make you want to die.

Phase Two: Pair another chore alongside the one you're currently doing. If you're dusting, have your daily load of laundry in the washer. If you're folding laundry, you have the dishwasher going.

Part Three: Always pair the same tasks, so that you create a type of ritual you will start doing without thinking about it. If you always start a load of laundry before you start dusting, you'll naturally flow into that cleaning rhythm. It's one less thing to think about when you're cleaning.

Deep Clean the House Once a Week

Depending on the size of your space, you shouldn't need to spend much more than an hour a week on cleaning if you do the 10-minute maintenance run each day. Use this time for the deeper cleaning. Listen to a podcast and make this cleaning time a spiritual practice where you can zone out and get excited about your super clean space.

Make a New Weekly Cleaning Routine for Your Minimalistic Space

Perform A Mandatory Weekly Sweep: Continue picking up items throughout your home daily and place them in their appropriate spaces. The only task you should need to do is sweep and possibly an intermittent mopping if needed. Once a week, do a quick 30-minute cleaning. If you have roommates, get everyone involved. The floors should take less than ten minutes. If you have younger kids, let them dust the furniture.

Do A Thorough Dusting: You already know how quickly the dust can accumulate on surfaces. Just take the time to really dust your home with a special cleaner; not just a dry cloth or dusting wand.

Mop The Floors: Your floors will still require a thorough mopping weekly even if you have swept daily. The floors will look much nicer and be much cleaner. You will have less stress, especially if you're paddling around barefoot!

Make the Kitchen Sparkle

Consider these pointers for your kitchen:
1. *Clean-as-you-go:* Remove any messes, as they are made. Discipline yourself since it only takes about a minute or two to wash a few items. Get everyone in on the plan.
2. *Clear the Counters:* As with the floors, maintain your clutter and keep the counters clear except for essentials such as the coffee-maker and toaster. Wipe the surfaces once or twice each day.
3. *Weekly Spruce-up:* During your 30-minute cleaning session, not only do you sweep the floors, but also do a more thorough wipe-down of the rest of the kitchen. As a weekly cleaning, it won't take much effort to keep it clean.

Thoroughly Clean the Refrigerator: Inside & Out:
- Discard all of your leftovers the evening before your trash is scheduled for collection. Most leftovers are spoiled after three days.

- Wipe down all surfaces after the leftovers are extracted. Check for expiration dates of all leftover items to ensure it's all still healthy to consume.

Sort & Organize the Dishes
- In case you aren't aware, it's cheaper to run your dishwasher during the night time. The electricity is at a cheaper rate since it isn't prime time (5pm-9pm).
- Load your dishwasher before bed and set it to run at a later time. *(Many dishwashers have a 4-hour delay option.* Put the items in the cabinets the morning or after sorting your mail when you get home after work.

Laundry Extras
Several options work well for this task:
You should wash a minimum of one load of laundry each day. It will depend on the size of your family.
1. *Weekly or bi-weekly*: You can choose to take your oversized loads to the laundromat and get it all done in about 1.5 hours. It could save tons of time. Just bring them home to hang and put away.
2. *Wash All of the Bedding: Your b*edding should be washed at least weekly.
3. *Wash the Blankets & Throw Pillows:* You can clean pillows by tossing them in the washing machine or by vacuuming. Be sure to read instructions on the label before cleaning. Most blankets can be cleaned in the washing machine.

Tidy the Bathrooms
The bathroom can get pretty gross if you don't remain diligent. Try this process:

1. *Bi-weekly Cleaning:* If you keep things clean in the bathroom on a daily basis, all you need to do is a quick once-over every other week or so.

2. *Clean-As-You-Go:* It just takes a minute to wipe up a dirty bathroom sink or to give your toilet a quick swish-and-flush with the toilet brush. Scrub the shower just before you shower. Just do this when you see dirt.

Observe Kids' Toys
It's impossible to keep things perfectly clean when you have kids. Just use your minimalist approach:

1. *Use Baskets:* It's important to have plenty of baskets and other such containers. When it's time to clean up, just toss the stuff in.

2. *Quick Clean-Ups:* Throughout the day, messes are made, and we ask them to do a quick clean-up. It'll be messy again in 10 minutes, but at least it's a manageable mess. At the end of the day, the last clean-up lets us have some quiet time with a clean house.

Tidy the Office

Make a habit to daily sort any paperwork or mail or paperwork. You won't dread piles of paperwork accumulating which could take hours to sort. It only takes a minute of your time and helps keep countertops as well as your mind clear of clutter.

Yard Work Challenges

If you have a huge yard, it's nice for the kids to play in, but a hassle to maintain.

You do have a few choices:

If you just don't have the time or energy to keep the yard up by yourself, consider hiring someone for the task. You can still do some of the hobby-type work with minimal effort. Consider your budget, but it would surely clear your mind.

In essence, you should own just a few plants and only ones that can maintain themselves and no junk. The less you have in your yard, the better. Try a Zen-like rock or gravel garden instead of grass. Be a naturalist and let the grass go wild (just kidding).

Your Monthly Minimalist Cleaning Routine

Clean the Carpeting: If you can't wash your carpet, just sprinkle (using equal parts) with some borax and baking soda over your carpet and let sit for two to three hours. Vacuum it up and enjoy!

Wash or Spruce-Up The Curtains: They accumulate dust the same way your blinds do. Just be careful and read the directions before you clean them. Some can be tossed in the washing machine and dryer, while others may just need to be wiped with a damp cloth.

CHAPTER 16
Natural Cleaning Supplies

You have the opportunity to clean your house top to bottom using professional tips, why not have special cleaning supplies for the task? Your question is answered in this segment. You will have the supplies to clean and a few suggestions using natural oils to deliver a tantalizing aroma to your minimalist home.

You want to be sure your minimalist home can be enjoyed to its fullest if all surfaces are clean and shiny. As previously mentioned, the term minimalist means different things to different people. It is much better on your budget if you make your own products and know how to use them. You have the peace of mind, knowing you and your family are in a safe environment.

Cleaning Containers for Homemade Supplies

Before you get started, it's essential to store all of your cleaning products securely. Choose a space such as the top of a closet or consider putting a safety lock on the cabinet in case you have a youngster who likes to explore. These are just a few of the items you will need:

Buckets: If you need to do more than a spot clean, you will need a bucket or two. If you use a mop, a mop bucket would be needed. Otherwise, a smaller bucket will come in handy for cleaning other areas such as baseboards. You must be diligent with a toddler lurking. If you have a toddler, chances are you would like to remain within your spending range for household cleaners.

Spray bottle or two (glass is preferred): You will be mixing many chemicals that may need different types of containers. It is best to purchase high-quality containers, but if you're on a budget, Dollar General will have one or two to choose from in stock.

Plastic Containers with Lids: Ziploc-type containers are an excellent choice with its secure lid. Just make the chosen cleaner mixture is clearly marked for future use. Some products will have a shelf life.

Shaker Containers: Choose a container with a tight-fitting lid when possible. Save a parmesan cheese container or make your own using another option of choice.

Caddies or Tool Containers: You will need to corral your tools and cleaners in a caddy that will easily fit in a closet or pantry that is out of reach of children. Store them in spaces where the most clean-up is needed.

Natural Cleaning Products

Baking Soda: Toss the Comet and Ajax aside by using a portion of baking soda. It is good from scrubbing the toilet, to the sparkling carpet, and everything in between. It is also a great deodorizer and natural air freshener.

Distilled White Vinegar: You will achieve a natural disinfectant which is safely mixed using a one-to-one ratio with water. Use it to clean the cabinets, countertops, and floors as a great grease cutter. It's awesome for cleaning stainless fixtures. Spray the mixture onto your rugs or carpets. If you don't like the smell of it, just open the windows for the air to clear. Instead of purchasing an expensive product for the dishwasher such as Jet Dry, add a little vinegar into the cycle. Consider adding it to your laundry cycle in the place of regular fabric softener.

Vinegar Clean-Up in a Bottle: If you prefer a spray bottle; all you need is a solution of three parts of water to one part of vinegar. Use it for any cleaning job from shining windows to the garbage disposal.

Cleaning Tip Warning: Don't use vinegar on colored fixtures or brass; it might cause discoloration.

Vinegar for Limescale: The white spots in your sink are lime deposits from mineral-rich hard water. Try this formula to clean the surfaces:
1. Soak a paper towel with vinegar.
2. Wrap the towel around the spotted area.
3. Wait for ten minutes.
4. Buff dry with a paper towel.

Hydrogen Peroxide: Add a sprayer nozzle to a bottle of peroxide since the elements can break down when exposed to sunlight. Use a one-to-one ratio of water and peroxide if you want it diluted further. Spray down all of the countertops in the bath and kitchen areas to kill germs. You can also use hydrogen peroxide to remove stains including juice, blueberries or other berries, and blood.

Rubbing Alcohol: Ethanol or isopropyl alcohol is a common ingredient used in rubbing alcohol. The fumes are powerful, so be sure to use in a well-ventilated space. The fumes are also flammable, but it is excellent as a disinfectant and works as a great solvent for dissolving oil and dirt.

Stainless-Steel Cleaner: Use a soft cloth to wipe any surfaces going with the grain to remove fingerprints.

A Super Disinfectant: Combine one part each of water and rubbing alcohol into a spray bottle. Clean any germ-ridden spaces as well as your personal items, including thermometers and your earring posts.
1. *Sponge & Cloth Refresher*: Saturate the cloth with alcohol in a bowl to stand for about ten minutes. Rinse it, and you're done—no more stressing over the bacteria traveling.
2. *Sinks & Chrome Cleaner:* After you're done with the sink for the day; just spray a bit on the surface to clean, disinfect, and shine. Buff the basin and fixtures with a dry cloth. It can also be used on brass
3. *Sofa Stains*: The alcohol won't penetrate the fabric, and it will also evaporate quickly. Spray over the stained area and wipe with a clean sponge. Let it dry. If it feels matted, brush the spot using a soft bristle brush using a circular motion.

4. *Disinfect Your Keyboard, Mouse, phones, and remotes.* The degreaser and disinfectant elements will dry - almost instantly.

Borax: Borax is made of Boron, which is an essential mineral the body actually needs to function correctly but, just like with most things, in excess, it can be harmful. Is it safe? You <u>can</u> decide.

Liquid Castile Soap: If you find vinegar offensive, use this soap as a great multipurpose cleaner. Use it as a personal care product and cleaning. Add a bit of water and tea tree oil for another multipurpose cleaner.

Microfiber Cloths: Purchase one of these cleaning cloths to clean your entire house (not the toilet). All you need is water to clean the surface. Choose a different color for each of your areas, so you don't cross contaminate.

Microfiber Cloth Mops: You can also purchase a chemical-free version of microfiber for a cleaning option using just water.

Squeegee: A squeegee will change the way you look at window cleaning. All you need to do is spray the chosen window cleaner on the window and away goes the grime. You can also purchase one that has a sponge attached if your outside windows are particularly dirty. Just dip the sponge in the cleaner bucket, scrub the window, and squeegee away the grime. You will need a couple of towels in the workspace to avoid spills or drips.

Sponges: You probably already have a stash of odor-free sponges that will work great with your new natural-cleaning products. You will also benefit with a Magic Eraser, a melamine sponge. It is best used by adding water first. If that doesn't remove the stubborn mark or dirt, just dip it in a little soapy water. You can also use your all-purpose cleaner with a little peppermint or lemon oil on a sponge mixed with warm water. Be sure to test a space before using the Magic Eraser to ensure it is safe.

Scrub Brushes: It's important to designate separate scrub brushes for particular jobs to avoid any cross-contamination. You can use a small toothbrush for small spaces such as around spigots (of course, a new one).

Broom & Mop: You will need the old-fashioned team, but just for quick clean-ups or spills. You can choose different types of mops, including a twistable mob, sponge mop—or my favorite, a refillable mop with microfiber pads. Just throw the pads in the washer for a sanitary clean the next time it's needed.

Dusting Wands: The best dusting wand to choose is one with a removable, washable duster. It should be capable of reaching the tall ceilings and corners with ease.

Vacuum Cleaner with Attachments: Select a high-quality vacuum that is within your budget. Be sure it has a good warranty. All you need to do is empty and clean the canister, or replace the bag often for the best results. Lastly, if your budget allows, a <u>wet/dry</u> vacuum could save you a ton of stress.

You will also use many other items, including:
- Lemons

- Natural salt
- Oven cleaner (see recipe)
- Bleach
- Wood polish (see recipe)
- Glass Cleaner (see recipe)
- An all-purpose cleaner (see recipe)
- Kitchen cleaner or wipes
- Rubber gloves
- Paper towels and cleaning cloths
- Toilet Brush
- Funnel

Special Cleaners
All-Purpose Cleaner
1. Fill a 32-ounce spray bottle up to an inch or two below the fill line. Leave room to add the soap and essential oil.
2. Add approximately 2 tablespoons of castile soap (peppermint, citrus or any scent you like or even unscented).
3. Add 10 to 20 drops of tea tree oil.
4. Shake gently to combine.
5. This cleaner can be used anywhere you would use a vinegar cleaner or any other conventional multipurpose cleaner around your house.

Glass Cleaner
This fabulous cleaner is great to have around for all those cute little fingerprints!
Items Needed:
- Water (2 cups - filtered or distilled)
- Essential Oil of choice (10 drops)
- Vinegar (2 tbsp.
- Spray bottle (glass is preferred)
- Microfiber cloth

How to Use:
1. Combine each of the fixings into the spray bottle.
2. Spray on your windows or any other glass surface using the fragrance of your choice; many use lemon-scented ones.

Lemon Household Cleaner
Items Needed:

- Water (8 oz.)
- Distilled white vinegar (4 oz.)
- Tea Tree Oil (15 drops)
- Lemon essential oil (15 drops)
- Glass - cleaning spray bottle

How to Use:
1. Fill the bottle with all ingredients and mix.
2. Shake the contents before each cleaning job.

Tip: It is advisable to use a glass container when possible. The citrus essential oils are highly concentrated and have acidic properties. Sometimes, it is best to store the products in glass for this reason.

Lemon Dishwasher Powder - Detergent
You want to be sure the food you serve your youngster is served on clean and sanitized dishes. You will get that with these amazing non-toxic chemicals.
Yields: 24 loads @ 1 heaping tbsp. per load
Items Needed:
- Baking soda (1 cup)
- Arm & Hammer Super Washing Soda (1 cup)
- Borax (1 cup)
- Lemon essential oil (20 drops)

Variations of Items Needed:
- *Unscented Product*: Leave out the essential oil
- *For Hard Water*: Add a ½ cup portion of Epsom salts.
- *Citrus Aroma*: Add 10 drops each of lemon and orange essential oils.
- *Peppermint & Lemon*: Use 10 drops of each oil.

How to Prepare:
1. Combine the components in a large mixing bowl.
2. *To Use:* Put one heaping tablespoon per load in the dish detergent compartment. Run as usual.
3. *To Store:* Pour mixture into a glass bottle or other container with a lid. Dress it up with an antique colored canning jar. It will keep the mixture dry until it's needed.

Lemon & Clove Liquid Dish Soap
Lemon and clove are fresh scents to include in your kitchen tools. The combination will make your dishes streak-free and sparkling clean.
Items Needed:
- Lemon essential oil (10-15 drops)

- Citrus castile soap/unscented castile soap (8 oz.)
- Clove essential oil (5 drops)

Variations of What You Need:
- *Citrus:* Substitute lime, orange, or grapefruit for the clove.
- *Grease Fighter:* Add a splash of white vinegar to the warm dishwater.

How to Prepare:
1. Pour the soap and oils into a storage container and shake well.
2. *To Use:* Add 1-2 squirts to the dishwater and scrub away.
3. *To Store:* Store on the counter or safely away from your toddler's reach.

Lemon Juice for Stubborn Stains

If you have a stubborn sink stain; try this remedy:

Items Needed:
- Powdered Borax (½ Cup)
- Lemon Juice (juiced - ½ of 1)

How to Clean:
1. Use a sponge to dab the mixture, rub, and rinse with hot water.
2. The method works well on stainless steel, porcelain, enamel, and many others.

Soft Abrasive Cleaners

If you prefer using a product such as Soft Scrub to clean your porcelain sinks or similar spaces, you can use a natural source without using bleach.

How to Clean:
1. Get the sink wet.
2. Sprinkle a portion of baking soda on the surfaces.
3. Use a cleaning rag to clean the surface until the sink or other surface is sparkling.

Scouring Powder

Items Needed:
- Salt - not iodized (.5 cup)
- Washing <u>soda</u> (.5 cup) Ex. Arm & Hammer
- Baking soda (1 cup)
- Optional: Lemon essential oil (5 drops)

How to Clean:
1. Pour the components into a bowl or jar.

2. Mix well and store in a shaker.
3. If you do not have a shaker, use a jelly jar and punch holes in the top.
4. Clean it using the concoction whenever you have a stubborn stain.

Tip: For tougher surfaces, apply undiluted white vinegar and water to the surface. Sprinkle the powder on the surface to sit for about five minutes. Scrub with a sturdy brush and rinse with vinegar and water.

Natural Toilet Bowl Scrubber - Deep-Clean
Items Needed:
- Vinegar (1 cup)
- Borax (.75 cup)
- Tea Tree essential oil (.5 tsp.)
- Lemon essential oil (5 drops)

How to Use:
1. Combine all of the ingredients in a medium glass container.
2. Measure the portions (¼-½ cup) in the toilet bowl. Let it sit for several minutes.
3. Use a brush to remove the stains.

For a Spray: You can also make it a bit thinner to use as a spray.
For a Scrub: Add a ¼ cup portion of baking soda to the mix and use gloves to scrub the toilet.

Natural Homemade Drain Cleaner
You don't need to purchase a bunch of fancy cleaning products for maintaining a clean and clear drain. Use one of these simple solutions:

Product 1: *Clear The Drain*
Items Needed:
- Baking Soda (.75 cup to 1 cup)
- Vinegar (.5 cup)

How to Clean:
1. Pour the baking soda in the drain.
2. Pour the vinegar into the drain and immediately cover the drain.
3. Leave everything to sit and work for about 30 minutes, but don't use the sink during this time.
4. After 30 min., run hot water through the pipes for about 2 to 3 min.
5. For really tough clogs you may need to repeat, but if you do this on a regular basis (about once a month) it keeps my drains clear and fresh without any problems.

Product 2: *Simple Drain Freshener*

Items Needed:

- Baking Soda (1 cup)
- Cream of Tartar (¼ cup)
- Salt (1 cup)

How to Clean:
1. Make a habit of pouring one-half cup of the mixture down the drain.
2. Pour a quart of boiling water in after you have added the mixture.
3. Do this every few weeks.

Homemade Natural Disinfectant Wipes
Items Needed:
- Wide-Mouth mason jar (1-quart size or 4-6 cup capacity & tight-fitting lid)
- Cleaning cloths - 10x10 squares (15-20)
- Filtered water (.75 cup)
- White distilled vinegar (.75 cup)
- Lemon essential oil (15 drops)
- Lavender essential oil (8 drops)
- Bergamot essential oil (4 drops)

How to Prepare:
1. Combine all of the fixings in a mason jar or other type of glass storage container. Note; the essential oils could have an adverse effect on plastic.
2. Swirl the components to combine.
3. Push the rags into the solution to soak. Securely close the lid and rotate the jar as needed to keep the rags moist.
4. Use any time for a quick clean up, so your toddler has a clean place for his/her precious cargo.

Natural Wood Cleaner
You don't want to take any chances with your table when cleaning it. This sounds almost good enough to eat:

1. Squeeze juice of one lemon into a small jar.
2. Pour in 1 tablespoon of olive oil.
3. Measure and pour in 1 tablespoon of water.
4. Thoroughly shake until it emulsifies.
5. Pour a small amount on a soft cloth and clean all of the wood furniture. This is also excellent if you have wood paneled rooms.

Dusting Spray for Cleaning Furniture
This is a fabulous choice to bring the luster back to your furniture. However, this mixture shouldn't be used on glass, walls, granite, or

stainless steel since it contains oil. Avoid using it on fine antiques or unfinished wood.

Items Needed:
- Vinegar (.5 cup)
- Water (1 cup)
- Oil of choice (2 tbsp.) ex. grapeseed, sunflower, or olive
- Cedarwood essential oil (5 drops)
- Lemon essential oil (10 drops)
- Brown amber bottle

How to Clean:
1. Pour the vinegar and water into a spray bottle.
2. Add in your oils and shake.
3. Cover the bottle and store.
4. Tip: A brown bottle is suggested since the essential oils are potent and could damage a plastic bottle over long periods of time.

Special Cleaner for Fabric Couches & Chairs

Items Needed:
- White Vinegar (1 tablespoon)
- Dish Washing Liquid (1 teaspoon)
- Warm Water (1 cup)
- Baking Soda (1 teaspoon)

How to Clean:
1. Baking soda is the base, and vinegar is the acid that creates carbon dioxide. The results are lots of cleaning bubbles.
2. Add the dish liquid into a spray bottle with the vinegar.
3. Pour in the warm water.
4. Combine the mixture over the sink. Add the baking soda, and quickly screw on the top of the sprayer.
5. Use the mixture to clean the entire surface of the couch.
6. Be sure it is thoroughly dry before you place any items directly on its surface.

Natural Air Freshener Spray

What You Need:

- Filtered water (6 tbsp.)
- Vodka (1 tbsp.)
- Essential oil (10 to 40 drops)
  (Citrus, Peppermint, Jasmine, & Lavender)

How to Use:
1. Place the alcohol and oils in a small spray bottle.
2. Shake well and add the water.
3. Shake before you spritz whenever you want to be energized.

Here are a few more versions using another method for sprays. Each is three ounces:

Fresh Floral:
- 4 drops Frankincense oil
- 8 drops Juniper oil
- 6 drops each:
- Jasmine oil
- Rosemary oil

Energy Boost:
- 20 drops Lemon EO
- 8 drops Eucalyptus EO
- 2 drops each:
- Cinnamon EO
- Peppermint EO

Sweet Citrus:
- 10 drops Lavender EO
- 8 drops Sweet Orange EO
- 4 drops each:
- Bergamot EO
- Vanilla EO

Lavender Linen (2 Ounce Size)
- 1 tsp. Witch Hazel
- 15 to 20 drops Lavender
- Almost 2 ounces distilled water
- 2-ounce dark spray bottle

How to Use:
1. Add the lavender, witch hazel, and distilled water.
2. Spray your linens and pillows for a tantalizing effect.

Gel Air Fresheners

You will be amazed when you see how simple this really is to make. Lemon and lavender are good for serenity.

What You Need:
- 1 packet Knox Gelatin
- ¼ cup Vodka

- 1 to 2 d. food coloring
- A ¾ cup of water
- 15 d. essential oil (Grade oils are okay for this process.)

How to Prepare:
1. Bring the water to boil in a small pan and add the gelatin pack.
2. Stir until it is dissolved. Allow it to cool at room temperature.
3. Pour into a small jar. Add the oil, vodka, coloring, and any decorative items.
4. Stir and place in the refrigerator until it is set.
5. You can have fun with this one by adding decorations in the gel. You can also add a wick to the bottom of the glass and make a gel candle.
6. *Note:* As the aroma fades—add a few more drops.

CHAPTER 17
Super-Clean — Specific Spaces

Super-Clean the Countertops & Backsplash:
If you have white countertops, a cleaner with bleach included or soft-scrub (see the recipe) can be used for stubborn stains. Be sure to follow the manufacturer's instructions, so you don't damage the surfaces. These are the basics for four common countertops:

Butcher-Block Countertops
Items Needed:

1. Warm, soapy water
2. A mild bleach solution
3. A non-abrasive kitchen cleaner

How to Clean:

1. Use a toothbrush along the edging to remove any debris.
2. If the surface feels tacky, use a baking soda and water paste.
3. Then, rinse thoroughly.

Marble Countertops
Cleaning marble countertops is a bit different. It should be cleaned regularly with a soft, damp cloth (microfiber works well) to prevent streaks. Rinse it thoroughly to remove any residue. Wipe it dry because air drying can create water spots.
If acidic foods stain the surface such as wine, orange juice, or tomatoes; you may need to have the professionals clean the spot.

Ceramic Tile Countertops

You can use soap and water to clean ceramic tiles, but you need to be sure to rinse them thoroughly because soap can leave a filmy residue behind. Add some vinegar to the water to alleviate this issue. Never use an abrasive pad or cleaner.
Note: Even though the tile doesn't stain easily—the grout will—with bacterial buildup as a result. Use a mild bleach solution and a toothbrush to clean the grout.

Concrete Countertops
Clean the surface with warm and soapy water. Rinse it thoroughly. You can use a mild bleach solution, but never use a scouring pad or abrasive cleaner on the surfaces.

For stubborn stains, make a paste of baking soda and water. You may also use talc mixed with a mixture of bleach, ammonia, or hydrogen peroxide. Apply the paste to the stained area, and use a soft brush to scrub the stain gently. Rinse thoroughly.

Super-Clean the Garbage Disposal

If you smell something that seems rancid, it could be the garbage disposal needs some cleaning also. Simply, grind a few lemons in the unit to make it fresh and clean. Repeat the process every few weeks. You can also sprinkle baking soda in the drain for several hours before running the disposal. For a deeper clean, use this method for the garbage disposal drain:

Items Needed:

- White Vinegar (1 Cup)
- Baking Soda (.5 cup)

How to Clean:

1. The mixture will fizz (remember pop rocks candy from the 1970s) with a popping noise.
2. Wait a few minutes.
3. Pour boiling water down the drain.
4. Fill the drain with 2 cups of ice.
5. Pour one cup of salt in the drain over the ice cubes (rock salt or sea salt is a good choice if you have it).
6. Turn the cold water faucet to the on position.
7. Turn on the disposal unit.
8. Run the disposal until the ice is gone.
9. The grime and debris should be loosened. Cut a lime or lemon in half and let the disposal chew them up for a deodorized drain.

Clean the Dingy Copper Pots

Copper pots hanging in a kitchen makes it have a charming, homey effect. Not only that, but it also saves a lot of space. However, you want to keep the surfaces shiny. Try one of these natural remedies that might surprise you:

- ***Catsup:*** Give catsup a whirl; it will look really gross, but the acid will help cut through the tarnished surface.
- ***Apple Cider Vinegar:*** Pour some AC vinegar into a paper plate and let it soak. Rinse the pan and dry it completely.
- ***Lemons & Salt:*** Cut the lemon into wedges; dip a wedge into the salt, and rub the pan until it's clean. Rinse the pan quickly and thoroughly in cold water, and wipe it dry.

- **Beer:** Put some beer on the pot. Let it sit for a couple of minutes. Rinse and wipe it until dry and shiny.
- **Cottage Cheese:** This is a cure that works without any scrubbing. Leave a layer of cottage cheese on the bottom for approximately five minutes. Rinse it completely and dry.

Don't Trash Your Favorite Mug

If you have stained coffee mugs, try this solution:
- Use sea salt or coarse salt mixed with a little lemon juice and scrub.
- Also, try baking soda and water made into a paste.
- This also works well on stained tea cups or coffee mugs, and even the cutting board.

Tackle the Oven Naturally

Use natural products to clean the oven manually. You can choose from several techniques for general cleaning of your oven.

Natural Oven Cleaner: Option 1: Simply apply a layer of baking soda and spray it with a vinegar solution. It should form a paste. Leave the mixture on the surface of the oven for five minutes. Wipe the oven with a damp rag or sponge.

Natural Oven Cleaner: Option 2: First, take a look at one of the general natural cleaning option using baking soda:

Items Needed:

- Baking soda
- Water
- Spray bottle

How to Clean:

1. Begin by spraying the oven with water until it's damp.
2. Sprinkle a ¼-inch layer of the soda, making sure you cover the entire surface.
3. If you see a dry spot, respray it with the water.
4. Let the mixture rest for at least three to four hours with the oven *OFF*.
5. Wipe the paste with an old towel to remove the grime.
6. It could take several applications, but thank goodness, it is natural.

Natural Oven Cleaner: Option 3: If you're in a hurry, this will help remove the stuck on grease and food.

Items Needed:

- Baking soda (3 tbsp.)
- Warm water (1 cup)
- Castile soap (1 tbsp.)

Variations:

- Lemon & Clove: Add 5 drops each.
- Lemon: Add 10 drops essential oil
- Lemon & Rosemary: Add 5 drops of each oil.

How to Clean:

1. Add all of the ingredients into a spray bottle. Shake well to mix.
2. *To Use*: Spray the oven liberally and let it sit for about 15 minutes.
3. Wipe it clean with a cloth or sponge. Rinse and let it air dry.
4. *To Store*: Store the leftovers for up to two weeks. Shake to combine before using.

Pamper the Bath Space

Many professionals recommend using disposable disinfecting wipes for the faucet and handle to reduce bacteria buildup greatly. Several studies provided facts indicating the bacteria found on the toilet set are some of the same germs tested in the kitchen sink.

What a terrible thought, but cross contamination can happen. If you use a cloth cleaning rag in the bathroom, be sure it doesn't get washed with the same towels used in your kitchen. Think of the vicious circle of bacteria, from the kitchen to the bathroom before you wash your hands!

Use toothpaste as a scouring agent or multipurpose cleaner. It will shine the faucet, remove crayons from the wall, and serve many other purposes. Think of that when you start getting to the bottom of the tube. Why not try it and be frugal? You might use it from then on!

The Ventilation Fan

The bathroom vent fan can sometimes be overlooked, and it's a huge mistake because it could be circulating a lot of dust and possible mold spores from the bathroom.

Step 1: The safest thing to do first is to trip the circuit breaker. Use a tool to remove the protective cover. Prepare a container of hot water with dishwashing soap and let the cover soak.

Step 2: Use the nozzle attachment on the vacuum cleaner to remove the gunk from the fan blades and other nooks and crannies. Use a clean paintbrush to remove the debris from the motor.

Step 3: Wash and rinse the cover.

Step 4: Replace the cover.

Super-Scrub for the Toilets

- Pour ¼ Cup Chlorine Bleach
  OR
- Pour ½ Cup White Vinegar into the bowl.

Don't use either product at the same time. Let the product used sit for about an hour. Brush the entire interior with the brush and flush.

Cleaner for Limescale: Sometimes, Coca-Cola will remedy the issue of limescale buildups. The cola's natural acids will breakdown the lime deposits. Pour the end of a glass of cola into the toilet, swish it around with the toilet brush, and see if it helps. The stains might be too deep, but many have reported the Coca-Cola does work!

However, at any rate, you can begin the cleaning process of the toilet by pouring a cup of baking soda into the toilet bowl. Let the soda soak for a few minutes. Use a stiff bristle brush and scrub the toilet as needed. Flush. If you still have some difficult spots, you probably need to use a damp pumice stone. It is abrasive but gentle enough not to damage the surface. The toilet brush should also be thoroughly cleaned after each use to prevent from spreading the bacterial germs. After you have cleaned the bowl, secure the handle of the brush between the bowl and the seat. Pour some bleach over the bristles and let it soak for a few minutes. Rinse it with a bucket of water.

It's essential to keep a clean toilet at all times. Imagine how the bowl releases particles/bacteria into the air each time it is flushed. It is similar to a fireworks display. If the bacteria linger, you could get sick from salmonella or E. coli as it flies around or lands on the handle and seat. It is best to close the lid before you flush. It is also best to store contact lenses and toothbrushes in the cabinet. Think about it; it's a risky health practice that has been performed for years. It's about time to change.

Super-Clean the Tub & Shower

Some heavy-duty products may be necessary to remove mildew stains and soap scum build-ups. If you have a shower caddy—it could be time for a replacement—or you can remove it and wash it. You can use a toothbrush for cleaning any small spaces such as the tub jets.

For the shower walls and sides of the tubs, use a mild abrasive and a sponge or cloth. Don't use a brush inside the tub because it can scratch the surface.

Tile Grout: Mix 1-part water and 3-part baking soda mixed into a paste. Apply to grout and let sit. Spray the area with a vinegar and water solution. Scrub with a toothbrush. After the cleaner finishes foaming; rinse with plain water.

For Deeper Stains: The nasty grout can be tackled with a mixture of 1-part bleach, 10-parts water, and a soft bristled brush.

Clean The Shower Head: Use an old toothbrush and bathroom cleaner (such as the new version of Soft-Scrub) to clean the shower head. If you have mineral deposits blocking the holes, you can soak the showerhead using a rubber band, a plastic bag, and white vinegar.

This method works well with heads made from stainless steel, chrome, or other protected metal surfaces.
1. Slip the rubber band over the top of the showerhead (loop the band around the arm at least twice so the bag will remain in place.
2. Wait for one hour.
3. Remove the bag and rinse with water.
4. Polish with a soft rag.

If the vinegar solution isn't sufficient, you will need to remove the showerhead for more extensive cleaning. Use the following process to make the job a little simpler:

Disconnect the Showerhead:

- Cushion your tool with a cloth as you work, so the surface finish is protected.
- Use a screwdriver to remove the nut at the shower arm.
- Rinse the showerhead under a faucet (upside down) to remove any loosened debris.
- Dismantle and clean the shower head. If you still see buildups; use a toothbrush, safety pin, or toothpick to poke out any leftover deposits.
- Soak the parts in vinegar overnight.
- Thoroughly rinse the showerhead in the morning.
- Reassemble and install the showerhead.
- Wrap new plumbing tape around the threads of the shower arm for a good seal.
- Reattach the head to the shower arm with a wrench.
- Use a soft towel or rag to prevent damage.

Towel Racks & the Hand Towels

Always use the sanitize setting on your washing machine or bleach the towels. Replace them every three or four days. Think of this as you are stripping the bathroom for its deep cleaning. Why not rewash all of the towels for a clean start?

Thoroughly clean the towel bar. If possible, don't install the towel rack near the toilet. Think of the germs, especially with a moist towel. In the future, be sure to use a towel bar so the towel can thoroughly dry. With a crumpled towel, the moisture can create bacteria.

Quick & Easy Ways to Refresh the Space

To finish off the bathroom space, choose a corner of the closet, and add a container of baking soda to help absorb any of the musty odors which can collect. Avoid using products, including Lysol or Febreze, because they do have a host of chemicals that could be harmful to you.

Essential Oils: (Optional) These are a few of the most popular scents to add to your cleaning products. Essential oils provide many benefits, but for now, the focus is on disinfecting and cleaning qualities. Be sure you purchase essential oils - not fragrance oils. However, the list is unlimited:

- Tea Tree Oil: Antifungal, antibacterial, antiviral, antiseptic & antimicrobial
- Eucalyptus: Deodorizer & anti-infective
- Lemon: Antiviral, anti-infective, antiseptic & antifungal
- Lime: Air Freshener
- Grapefruit: antiseptic & air freshener
- Clove: Air freshener
- Orange: Air freshener
- Lavender: Antifungal, anti-infective & antiseptic
- Peppermint: Antiviral, antiseptic, antifungal & Antibacterial
- Rosemary: Antiviral, antiseptic, antimicrobial, antifungal & antibacterial

Super-Clean the Carpeted Spaces

Use preventive maintenance to eliminate part of the dirt that can enter your home and become embedded into your carpet. Begin by arranging doormats in front of each of your home's entrances. Vacuum your carpeting at least twice each week to ensure your youngster cannot pick up any undesirable morsels. You also help control dust, dust mites, and other irritants. Invest in a strong vacuum with a HEPA filter.

Choose Nontoxic Alternatives

If you have small children, you will want to use a non-toxic, non-irritating alternative to chemical cleaners. Be sure to clean up spills using a cloth immediately. Don't rub; blot the spot. Try one of these solutions:
- Sprinkle baking soda, cornstarch or cornmeal over greasy stains.
- If you have a red wine stain, try a rag with plain club soda to help remove the spot.
- Help remove any sticky 'stuff' using a piece of ice. Scrape off hard substances with using a butter knife. Then, mix one cup of water with 1/2 teaspoon liquid dish detergent together or mix 1/3 cup white vinegar with 2/3 cup warm water. Spray with the mixture to clean the spot.
- Steam clean using plain water. For extra tough stains mix 1.5 cups of white vinegar with 2.5 gallons of water.

Steer clear of the cleaned carpet for at least six hours. Carpets that don't dry efficiently are prone to mildew, mold, and fungal growth. Open the windows for fresh air circulation and thoroughly vacuum the spot. For extra deodorizing, use a shaking of baking soda.

Avoid wet-washing the carpet on humid days. Use fans, pointing them directly them over damp carpeting. Choose products you know will be safe for your toddler, such as the ones described in this cleaning book of guidelines. After the carpet dries, just sprinkle with baking soda and wait a few minutes for it to absorb the odors. Vacuum as usual.

Carpet Freshener
Items Needed:

- Cinnamon Leaf essential oil (30 drops)
- Clove Bud essential oil (10 drops)
- Lemongrass essential oil (30 drops)
- Eucalyptus essential oil (30 drops)
- Bicarbonate soda/Baking soda (.5 cup)

How to Prepare & Use:

1. Simply blend all of the ingredients in a wide mouth jar.
2. Close the lid for 24 hours.
3. Add a sprinkle when the carpet needs refreshing, and leave it there for 10 to 15 minutes before you vacuum away the residue.

Super-Clean the Laundry Space
The Washer
Items Needed:

- White Vinegar (for a natural source) or Bleach
- Baking Soda
- Microfiber Cloth
- Tooth Brush

Step 1: Select the hottest water setting and fill the washer to the highest load size and the longest wash cycle.
Step 2: As the washer is filling, add one cup of bleach and one quart of white vinegar.
Step 3: Add one cup of baking soda. Close the washer's lid, and agitate for approximately one minute.
Step 4: Let the water, vinegar, and baking soda (or bleach) soak in the tub for about an hour. It is easy just to leave the top open.
Step 5: While the tub is soaking, remove any removable parts for a soak. Don't forget the bleach and fabric softener cups if they are removable. After they are rinsed and dried, you can replace them.

Step 6: Use a small brush such as a toothbrush to clean the topmost part of the agitator and other difficult spaces to reach spots.
Step 7: Make sure to clean the sides and the top of the machine lid.
Step 8: After one hour of soaking, close the lid, and let the cycle run its course.
Step 9: You can clean around all of the dials with a vinegar solution.
Step 10: Repeat one more hot wash with another quart of vinegar to clear away any loosened residue left from the first wash/rinse cycle.
Step 11: After the washer completes its cycle, wipe the bottom and sides of the washing tub with a vinegar mixture to remove any lingering residue.
Tip: Leave the lid open to allow a thorough drying out to prevent mildew.

Clean the Dryer

The first step is to remove the lint filter and give it a thorough cleaning. Use a duster in the filter well to retrieve the lint out of the trap. You can also use the vacuum cleaner's narrow wand/crevice tool for speedier cleanup time. Wipe all surfaces with a white vinegar solution.

Check the duct work behind the dryer. Use a vacuum to remove all of the lint and dust. Check the outside of the vent to be sure the flap can move freely. If not, the lint will block the vent and be a possible fire hazard.

Wash the exterior of the dryer with warm, sudsy water. Rinse the soap residue away by using a clean damp rag. Use a dry one to shine the surface.

Refresh the Clothes Washer and Dryer

Add one or two drops of oil into the washer (lemon and lavender are fresh aromas). Pour a bit of your chosen oil on a cloth and toss it in the dryer. It will make your clothes and the house have a wonderful smell.

Last but Not Least: Pamper Yourself

Homemade Liquid Hand Soap

It is best to purchase the items needed and make your own healthy formula to pamper your hands. After all, saving money with a high-quality product is what a minimalist home is all about.

Check these two options:

Option #1: Baby Mild Hand Soap

Items Needed:
- Pure castile soap (2- 5-ounce bars) ex. Baby Mild
- Distilled or filtered water (1 gallon)
- *Optional*: Vanilla extract or essential oils
- *Also Needed*: Large Pot

How It's Made:
1. Grate the soap bars until you have a large pile of shredded soap.
2. Warm up your water in a very large pot. Let it boil if you aren't using distilled water. Lower the setting and let it cool (hot, not boiling).

3. Stir in the soap chunks. Keep stirring until all the little flakes are dissolved.
4. Remove the mixture from the heat. Let it sit for 12 to 24 hours. The mixture will thicken during this time. Stir occasionally throughout the day.
5. Stir in your essential oils or vanilla extract, if using. Start small and put in enough until you get the right amount of aroma for you.
6. Pour the mixture into containers. This will make quite a bit. I was able to fill three soap dispensers and five other fairly large storage containers.
7. Enjoy your toxic-free, frugal, and easy homemade liquid hand soap.

Option #2: Simple Liquid Hand Soap
What You Need:
- Liquid castile soap - Your favorite
- Filtered or Distilled water
- Optional: Foaming Soap dispenser

How to Prepare:
1. Combine the fixings.
2. Fill a soap dispenser with a small amount of liquid castile soap; roughly 1 tablespoon.
3. Adjust the amounts depending on how thick you like your soap.

Minimalistic Bugs No More

Nothing is more worrisome than to be bothered by a mosquito. You can keep them away naturally without commercial chemical products. Forget those pricey products that don't work.

Healthy Bug Repellent Lotion Bar

This is what you need:

- Organic Coconut Oil (.25 cup)
- Castor Oil (.125 cup)
- 10 drops each of:
  - Eucalyptus Oil
  - Citronella Oil
  - Clove Bud Essential Oil
- .33 cup each of:
  - Raw Cocoa Butter
  - Beeswax pellets

How to Prepare:

1. Put the pellets, castor oil, cocoa butter, and coconut oil in a heavy-duty saucepan using the medium heat setting.
2. Once all of the oil, butter, and wax are melted; remove from the burner to cool (3 to 4 minutes).
3. Blend in the essential oils.
4. Empty it into a preferred mold, tin or jar

Suggestion: A basic soap mold will do the trick. Be sure the container can handle the hot product. Cut the bars into chunks and place in a decorative container.

Directions for Use:

1. Rub the bar between your hands to help the solution melt enough to rub gently over your exposed skin.
2. You will receive a pleasing smell which is so mild; it's safe for your children.

Bug Spray: Option 1

What You Need:

- Boiled or distilled water
- Natural witch hazel
- Choose from Clove, Lemongrass, Tea Tree, Citronella, Cajuput, Cedar, Eucalyptus, Catnip, Mint, or Lavender.
- *Optional*: Vegetable glycerin

How to Prepare:

1. Fill an 8-ounce bottle half full of water.
2. Add the witch hazel and ½ tsp. of vegetable glycerin (if used).
3. Add 30 to 50 drops of the chosen scent.
4. *Note*: Remember when the oils are increased, you are also increasing the aroma.

Bug Spray: Option 2

What You Need:

- Emulsifier (1 tsp.)
- Vinegar (4 oz.)
- Eucalyptus (50 drops)

- 25 drops each of:
  - Spearmint
  - Lemon

How to Prepare & Use:

1. Blend the essential oils in a spray bottle with the emulsifier, and the vinegar.
2. Shake well to mix.
3. Spray around the baseboards to keep the bugs away.

Bug Repellent: Option #3 for a Cold Air Diffuser

What You Need & Instructions:

1. 1 drop of each essential oil: Lemongrass |thyme |basil |eucalyptus
2. Add about 70 ml of water.
3. Combine each of the ingredients.
4. Use as desired.

"The secret of happiness, you see, is not found in seeking more, but in developing the capacity to enjoy less." —Socrates

CONCLUSION
Maintain A Minimalistic Viewpoint

"Simplicity is the glory of expression." —Walt Whitman
The process of decluttering enables you to remove 10% of your items but also remove 10% of the budget. Live frugally. Once again, be honest—will you miss that small number of belongings? However, you must realize that clutter is present in many forms. You find it on daily 'to-do' lists, on your email account, and the Internet with mindless scrolling. You are cluttering your mind as well—good or bad—it distracts you from your personal goals. Keep only one (1) credit card—or maybe two. The card can be used as a financial tool, but be careful not to overspend. Remember that you will be paying interest on the money when you make the purchases. Even if it is a sale item, the interest payments may exceed the sale price. Think twice! This is a vital step toward becoming debt-free.
Appreciate what you have, and get organized. According to the National Association of Professional Organizers, in your lifetime, you will spend approximately one year looking for items—just one more reason to live with fewer items to clutter your home and your mind.
Clean up as you go, and only touch it once! Both of these make everything much easier. Cleaning up as you cook makes cleaning up after eating much quicker, especially if the dishwasher is empty. The dishes won't be piling up in the sink—but rather be put in the dishwasher ready to be cleaned.
Find a supportive group of people who understand your challenges as you prepare your home using the minimalist approach. By having an intentional community to provide you with encouragement and support during your journey will surely increase your success rate.
It is a learning process, and you will make mistakes. Practice the guidelines and stay in touch with your personal style. Carefully and intentionally are the best advice you can receive when it comes to shopping. It is difficult to stop the old habits of impulsive purchasing items, but with practice, you can improve. You will soon discover—living with less is much less stressful!
While it may seem that reducing clutter in your life is an impossible task, you absolutely can do it! Just take baby steps—start right now by addressing your own belongings. Find a support group and challenge each other!
Try it now—visualize what your life could be at the end of your journey. Imagine how your home can look with fewer items cluttering all of its surfaces. Think of the ways you could spend the time if you don't have a stack of dirty laundry or a pile of discarded toys laying around your space. Stay motivated and remove those unhappy visions. It will help you get through the tough times.
Finally, if you found this book useful in any way, a review on Amazon is always appreciated!

DESCRIPTION

Don't be confused because *Minimalist Home* includes all family members—no question about that! Simplifying family life should be a quest for the entire family. These are the topics you will learn more about minimalistic behavior:

- Minimalism Mindsets & Habits
- What Minimalism Is & Isn't
- Making a Plan
- Declutter & Organize the Kitchen
- Declutter the Dining Area
- Declutter & Organize the Bath Area
- Declutter the Living Room
- Revamp the Office
- Reorganize the Bedrooms
- For Kids Only: Minimalism
- Declutter Laundry Spaces
- Clean & Organize Spare Storage Areas
- Methods of Containment & Removal
- Benefits of a Minimalistic Home
- The Minimalist Mindset
- The Minimalist Plan for Home Maintenance

Each of these topics are fully explained, so you will soon understand the theories involved with minimalist behavior and how to maintain your home.

"It is always the simple that produces the marvelous." —Amelia Barr

www.ingramcontent.com/pod-product-compliance
Lightning Source LLC
Chambersburg PA
CBHW071506070526
44578CB00001B/461